A CLASSIFIED LOOK AT THE GREAT SATAN OF AMERICA

TOP SECRET GOVERNMENT PERSECUTION

By Mark C. Russell

1, 1235 64 Avenue SE
Calgary, AB, Canada T2H 2J7
www.blitzprint.com

Distributed to the trade by Ingram Books

CONTENTS

PREFACE

BOTTOM LINE: Simply, **The Great Satan of America** or Satan's system, will devour you into his system by force or you will be put to death. In other words, you compromise with Satan's system or he will either make you very sick, pain stricken, or injured to the point of forcing you into his system. Ultimately, if you don't compromise with Satan you will be put to death by any means possible. Satan's system involves the forceful pressures of every facet of mental, physical, political, social, economic, psychological, and religious entities. All systems globalwide; government, civilian, religious (Satanic, Christian, or Otherwise), or other, are all subject to Satan's System.

In my book I cover the U.S. Government, the Judges, the Court System, the Jail System, the Attorneys, the Mental Health System, and the Workman's Compensation Hearing. I cover how they all interact to what I call Satan's system whereby Satan is considered **"the lawless one"**. I believe it's the beginning to Satan's rise to power during what the Bible calls the beginning of the Tribulation Period (the End of The Ages).

Ultimately, if not put to death you will forcibly (per entities above) become possessed by demonic beings. And, your life will be subject to the underhanded possession of demonic interests. Plainly, these demonic beings constantly talk to you and control what you say and control your physical actions as well. Satan highly secrets these truths; either forcefully, by possibly putting you into psychiatric care or an institution, making you injured, or making you very sick/pain stricken, or putting you to death. Again, this is a compromising system; you simply compromise with Satan and he will highly regard you. God says not to compromise. Accordingly, our church is presently and is classified as the **Laodicean** church, neither not nor cold (e.g. lukewarm) and God spits us out of his mouth (Per bible, the book of Revelation 3:16).

I believe Satan is actively seeking me (and every Christian or Gentile) per 1 Peter 5:8 which says, "... Your enemy the devil prowls around like a roaring lion looking for someone to devour." I've even had a family member with a license plate number containing 666. During 2003, in the

Brockport, NY and surrounding areas, I saw cars containing 666 license plates on dates 1-12,1-15,1-18,1-21,1-23,1-27, 2-06,3-31, 4-04, and 4-16. During 2004, I saw cars containing 666 license plates on dates 1-21,1-23, 3-16, 4-29, 5-05, 5-24, 5-26, 6-23,7-30, 8-05, 8-26, 9-09, 11-11, 11-22, and 12-15. And during 2005, I saw cars containing 666 license plates on dates 1-02, 1-04, 2-13, 2-14, 4-25, 7-11, 7-31, 9-16, 10-03, 10-08, 11-19, and 11-23. Satan is letting people know that he is the Prince of this world (e.g. John 12:31). Per Revelation 13:16-18 reads, "He also forced **everyone**, small and great, rich and poor, free and slave, to receive a mark on his right hand or on his forehead, so that no one could buy or sell unless he had the mark... His number is 666." The system I'm describing is how Satan will come to power. He possesses people demonically.

You are probably already saying how can so many people **today** be actively demonically possessed and living under the **secret** authority of Satan? Please read Ephesians 6:11 & 12 as follows: "...take your stand against the devil's schemes. For our struggle is not against flesh and blood, but against the rulers, against the authorities, against the powers of this dark world and against the spiritual forces of evil in the heavenly realms." Also, Mathew 10:36 says, "...a man's enemies will be the members of his own household." Present times dictates these points. Satan is also called the **"Deceiver "** and you are presently being deceived. What I'm saying is that in Jesus's day there were "many" demon-possessed individuals and that today there are very much more demon-possessed individuals spread globally. These demon-possessed individuals (which may include family, friends, coworkers, the church, or anyone or means) are carefully and forcefully recruiting many others into Satan's System by any and every possible means; including the means of evil supernatural forces (which you ultimately end up demon-possessed as well). The following are Bible verses relative to Demonic possession (several of these bible verses say **"many"** demons are involved; why can't there be **"many"** demons involved today -- spread globally?: **Mathew** 4:24 "...the demon-possessed...", 8:16 "...many who were demon-possessed...", 9:32 "...a man who was demon-possessed...", 10:1 "...authority to drive out evil spirits...", 10:8 "...drive out demons.", 11:18 "...he has a demon.", 12:22 "...brought him a demon-possessed man...", 12:24 "...that this fellow drives out demons...", 12:28 "But if I drive out demons...", 12:43 "When an evil spirit comes out of a man...", 15:22 "...suffering terribly from demon-possession.", 17:18 "Jesus rebuked the demon and it came out of the boy...".**Mark** 1:23 "...who was possessed by an evil spirit...", 1:27 "He even gives orders to evil spirits...", 1:32 **"...** brought to Jesus all the sick and demon-possessed.", 1:34 "He also drove out many demons...", 1:39 "...preaching in the synagogues and driving out demons.",

3:11 "Whenever evil spirits saw him, they fell down...", 3:15 "...to have authority to drive out demons.", 5:2 "...an evil spirit came from the tombs to met him.", 5:8 "...come out of this man, you evil spirit.", 6:13 "They drove out many demons...", 7:26 "She begged Jesus to drive the demon out of her daughter.", 7:29 "...the demon has left your daughter.", 9:17 "...my son, who is possessed by a spirit...", 9:38 "...we saw a man driving out demons...", 16:9 "...to Mary Magdalene, out of whom he had driven seven demons.", 16:17 "In my name they will drive out demons...". **Luke** 4:35 "Then the demon through the man down...", 8:2 "...some women who had been cured of evil spirits...", 8:27 "...Jesus stepped ashore he was met by a demon-possessed man...", 8:29 "...Jesus had commanded the evil spirit...", 9:1 "...he gave them power and authority to drive out all demons...", 9:42 "But Jesus rebuked the evil spirit...", 9:49 "...we saw a man driving out demons...", 10:17 "...Lord, even the demons submit to us in your name.", 10:20 "...do not rejoice that the spirits submit to you...", 11:14 "Jesus was driving out a demon...", 11:24 "When an evil spirit comes out of a man...", 13:10 "...who had been crippled by a spirit for eighteen years.", 13:32 "...go tell that fox, I will drive out demons...". Also, Adolph Hitler and his top officials were demon possessed but did you ever see Hitler and his officials foam at the mouth and unusually scream or act unusual as is what the general population believes demon possessed people do. Another example similar to Hitler and his top officials was Egypt's Pharaoh and his top officials (e.g. demon possessed). **None of these demon possessed people acted unusual (i.e. foam at mouth and screaming).** Again, why can't there be **"many"** demon possessed people today (who act normal) as is Satan's system is a heavily kept secret even to the point of death.

For example, take the **Figure Skating Profession**, in my opinion, takes on a typical Satanic oppressed system where Ekaterina and Sergei Gordeeva, Sergei died of a heart attack. You've probably heard of other heart attack notables like football and basketball players (a recent incident was a high-school basketball player being recruited by The University of Kentucky and died on the basketball court of a heart attack). Scott Hamilton has cancer. Maria Butyrskaya was threatened by a car bomb. And do you remember the Tonya Harding and Nancy Kerigan saga of 1994.

Another brief system involves **Golf's** John Daly and Fred Couples as being very emotional, Tom Lehman is very religious, and Jeff Sluman had his appendix out. Another note, was Monica Seles (Professional Tennis Player) was knifed in her back; and, John MacEnroe, constantly bellyaching.

From 1986-1989 I worked for the Defense Contract Audit Agency (DCAA) and did some Naval Top Secret auditing contracts. I was **illegally** being surveillanced, phones tapped, followed, and harassed ((1986-87) I worked in Annapolis, MD and 1987-89 I worked in Rochester, NY). Over a period of several years, after working for DCAA, **I was arrested five different times. The first four times I pleaded guilty to a lesser charge** and nobody heard about the **illegal** Satanic Government system. This **illegality** was in effect swept under the rug. I wanted to file a civil suit against the Government and could not find any Attorney to take the job (if I could find an Attorney court costs would be at least $10,000 of which I did not want to spend). I could not even get the TV or newspaper to write or do a clip or article. The fifth time arrested I had a jury trial and told some, **not complete**, my Satanic Government **illegal** episode. I could not find justice or redress to these Government law breaking activities. I still rightfully feel helpless.

Finally, **The Great Satan of America** (our Government) is breaking International Law (Top Secret Classified Information) ...The U.S.'s world's "deepest" going submarines are in Russia's Sea of Okhotsk looking at Russian rocket wreckage and tapping telephone cable lines. *Ultimately, I would like somebody, anyone, to help me sue the Government for both my emotional distress, paranoia, and disability in working.*

CHAPTER 1

Top Secret Employment With The Defense Contract Audit Agency (DCAA) 1986-1989

From 23 January 1986 to 13 August 1987 I worked for the Department of Defense in a TOP SECRET environment called Field Detachment in Annapolis, Maryland at Westinghouse (Oceanic Division). This TOP SECRET Satanic environment was part of the declassified organization called the Defense Contract Audit Agency (DCAA). We audited **TOP SECRET Navy Government Contracts. During this period my life was threatened (See Note No. 1 below).**

In October 1987 I transferred to Rochester, NY where we did not require high security. The transfer was because I felt the Government was **illegally** spying on me (e.g. tapping phones, surveillancing, and following me). Noted,illegal surveillance is a felony. Our Government are felons. A psychiatrist said I had paranoia but I know better. Another psychiatrist said differently. I believe everybody is spied on **illegally** in this organization at all times subject to the Agency's discretion. Because of their Satanic system **(The Great Satan of America)** I believe they have been **illegally** harassing me. What I would like is two fold: (1) let the public know that our Government is **illegally** invading peoples privacy and, *(2) help me sue the Government for both my emotional distress, paranioa, and disability in working.*

By Mark C. Russell

THINGS COWORKERS SAID DURING 1986-87 (EXCEPT Nos. 14-16 BELOW is 1989)

DCAA – Field Detachment @ Westinghouse Annapolis, MD

The following are things that coworkers said to me (which affected me emotionally with Paranioa and Anxiety) while I worked for the Government between the years 1986-1989:

1   Coworkers (Bobby and Sam) told me if I did not conform to the system the Contractor would bomb my car (this is plainly life threatening).

2   My Supervisor, **Mr. Davide**, told me not to even look for surveillance cameras in my house because I would never find them. They were so well hidden.

3   **Jack** (Coworker) told me that I should go to the Press concerning invasion of privacy.

4   The **whole office** would see films that would show you that the Government could ruin a person's life both financially and socially. The film would say things like the Government knows how many times you masturbate.

5   **Mr. Davide** (Supervisor) said to me and **Jack** (Coworker) that we had to keep a low profile and be aware of friends and neighbors that they may be spies.

6   I was told from **Elie** (Cameron Station – Field Detachment) that the Government was bugging my house even under my bed.

7   **Bobby** (Coworker) told me that the building we worked in had asbestos in it. This is in reference to being a health hazard.

8   **Sam** (Coworker) was talking about the Government using surveillance cameras on us and Sam said he "didn't mind a little man watching us."

9   **Bobby, Steve**, and **Mathew** all tried to pawn off **Harold's** wife on me.

10 **Harold** (Coworker) would carry pornographic movies in his briefcase and would bring this briefcase (pornographic movies included) to work where he was not supposed to.

11 **Harold** (Coworker), and a family man, had one of his lady flings call Harold at work identifying herself as **"Love Pool"**. This is indicative of Field Detachment employees!

12 **Steve** (Supervisor) would bring to work disco tapes and play them during work hours where he was not supposed to (breach of security).

13 **Steve** (Supervisor) told me I was lucky that I did not get kidnapped when I took a boat tour one night in Annapolis, MD.

14 **John** (1989 Coworker – Rochester, NY) used to work for Field Detachment and told me that these spies in the Top Secret Environment can spy on me any time they want to.

15 **Tammy** (1989 Supervisor – Rochester, NY) One day I heard conversation coming from Tammy's office to my desk location where Tammy was on her phone repeating what I had repeated on my phone before inside my apartment (this all happened within a weeks time). She repeated the phrase "shitty this, shitty that, and shitty everything" which Tammy got from me repeating this phrase on my apartment phone. I believe Tammy had the access/means to spy on me in and out of my apartment. This took place in 1989 where I was on the phone with a friend repeating the above quote which in turn Tammy repeated at the office. This, to me was proof positive that Tammy had a part in spying on me and she indirectly wanted to let me know this.

16 **Tim** (1989 Coworker – Rochester, NY) this is in reference, to be discussed later in this book, concerning the Government letting you know that they are illegally surveillancing/watching you by making noises in your home, car, and workplace. In reference to Tim, I was in his office (while the heating boards were making no noise) and then Tim went out of the room and instantaneously the heating boards (where I was sitting) started to make noises and when Tim came back into the room the heating boards instantaneously stopped making noises. I believe that Tim had access to these noise-making devices and as was Tammy (my Supervisor). I believe Tim had a part in spying on me and he indirectly wanted to let me know this.

17 **Harry** (Manager Field Detachment) was trying to **coach me** what to say " to whomever it may concern" while trying to move from Maryland back to Rochester, NY. He told me to say stuff like 'tell whomever that a good deal of your troubles is that of **no windows** in the workplace'. This was a bunch of bull anyway. Plainly, Harry's coaching was incorrect and he knew it was incorrect but wanted me to say it any way. Our staff had gotten outside every day during lunch.

CHAPTER 2

DCAA Government Invasion of Privacy And Trespass (1986-89) & (2002-2005) (A Good Conspiracy Is One That Can't Be Proven)

Since 1986, I believe that our **Satanic Government** has many times **illegally** invaded my privacy. Some glaring evidence of my plight concerning Invasion of Privacy and Trespass is as follows:

Baltimore, MD 1/86 to 8/87:

1   I noticed that things I said in my apartment were being repeated in the office. I tested my theory twice to see if my coworkers were spying on me. **First**, I repeated the phrase **"point of no return"** in my apartment and the next day I heard (from my peers) the same phrase. I did the same thing **again** but a different phrase giving the same results. I then had confirmed my suspicions that they were spying on me.

2   While at work one day I was on the phone with my doctor and I had asked him a private question. As I asked him this question I heard two people laugh on the other end of the phone line. It sounded like the two people that I had worked with (e.g. Bobby and Sam).

3   Many times I have heard the phone making a clicking noise as if the recorder was turned on and I also heard many times the volume of noise increasing and decreasing.

4   See **APPENDIX** concerning the environment I had to work with. You will see that Field Detachment as a **very disorganized** organiza-

tion where there was very little supervision, very little management oversight, and just minimal organization oversight (i.e. see the IG findings).

5   I had made a formal **GRIEVANCE (see APPENDIX – Reply to an Admonishment from Steve – Manager – Field Detachment)** which it was **never** answered.

6   The Government must of sprayed some kind of **fungus** (where my floor meets the wall) all around my brand new condominium. This never has taken place in any of the places I've lived in.

7   The **air**, in my condo, many times was filled with a dusty type component. It was to the point were I did not want to take this air in anymore. For approximately the last six months that I lived in my condo, I coughed every day all day long on and off (I believe the Government tampered with my home air system).

8   During the last six months in Maryland I had **hair loss** (just gobs of it). I believe this is just part of this Satanic/Government system.

9   My toilet would keep me up at night because my **brand new** toilet was broken. How did it get broken?

10   During my last two weeks in Maryland I woke up every night at exactly 12:30 am and had the runs (i.e. had to go to the bathroom).

11   The day I moved from Baltimore, MD to Rochester, NY one of my **brand new water pipes** (in my Baltimore condo) sprang a leak. It was leaking water. How did it get broke?

12   **James (Personnel Resources – DCAA - Field Detachment) Just before I moved from Maryland to New York James told me if I continued to seek litigation or the press or TV I would get a broken leg. I asked him what he meant by that and he said, "just that".**

13   One day driving to work (Westinghouse) a professional, I believe, car driver was heading straight dead on in my lane toward my car. I had to slam on my breaks and swerve off the pavement. I believe that the Government was trying to scare me so that I would condescend to their system. Nothing like this has ever happened to me. What a flagrant violation of **Human Rights**. I've had two car accidents since working for the Government. I believe the Government had something to do with these accidents!

14   One night a man and a woman knocked on my condo door. When I opened the door they both started to laugh. I don't know why they laughed but they were both trying to look into my condo. I asked what they wanted and they said they had the wrong address. They said they were supposed to go next door. I watched them leave and they just got into their car; they never went back next door. Why? I

believe the Government was specifically trying to **harass** me so that I would condescend.

15   Over several weeks, Jack (Coworker), kept on stating a blasphemous statement over and over by the author, "Dante". I believe he was actively trying to test my religious tolerance **(SPECIFIC HARASSMENT ON ME).** I had to specifically tell him to stop or he would have kept on his regimen!

16   During the last weeks while working for Field Detachment I listened to three different radio stations in my car going to and from work. All the songs that were played each contained lyrics that were evil as sorts (e.g. Witchy Woman, Lose Your Faith, Demons, Don't Belong Here In Heaven and continuous on and on). The point here is that I believe the Government was actively testing my religious tolerance **(SPECIFIC HARASSMENT ON ME)**. Condescension is the Government's priority even through high tech radio means. It's your word against their word.

17   Approximately after one year (while working for Field Detachment 1987) my coworkers every day constantly talked about HERPES. After several months into this a man moved into an empty room at our townhouse. In short, he told us (other renters) that he had Herpes. Thank God I did not use the same bathroom as he did. Being scared, I moved out of there the following week into my own place. About six months later, I moved back to New York. Right after I moved (to New York) I contracted a cold sore on my ass. Never before or to date have I ever contracted such a sore. I definitely believe that the Government played a part since day one!

Rochester, NY & Baltimore, MD 1988 – 89: (A Good Conspiracy Is One That Can't Be Proven)

1   Government made **many noises** in my house - crickets, birds, house rafters, dripping water faucet, water pipes, TV popping, lights ringing, etc..

2   **Government made lights blink:**
   a   I received a 1:30 a.m. phone call (in MD) from a friend (out of state friend) and on my way back from the kitchen (location of phone) to the bedroom, the lights blinked on and off. There was only a clear night out (no rain or storm).
   b   In Marta's (Therapist – in NY) office her lights blinked after I said something important concerning the Government.
   c   My lamp (in NY and MD) in my home blinked several times over the years. Couldn't figure out why.

d   While working for the Government in NY they had a blinking light above my desk that was not supposed to be blinking. It took about a month or more before they fixed it.

3   While moving from MD to NY I believe the Government had switched the **signal lights** hookup on the trailer of the car (i.e. Harassment); the day before the signal lights were working properly.

Rochester, NY 1988 – 89:
(A Good Conspiracy Is One That Can't Be Proven)

1   While working for the Government the Judge's **toilet water** on the floor above me overflowed and dripped on my desk.

2   While moving from MD to NY the Government put a **nail into my tire** while my car was in my driveway. A week after that my parents car also received a nail in the tire. This has never happened before this or to date.

3   While in NY, my first criminal act, **two transport officials** took me from jail to Triage and then to the Forensic Unit. While waiting to enter the Forensic Unit Transport Officer, **MS. Flippo**, got a pistol (gun) out of the glove compartment and flashed it in front of me **(scaring me to death)** and then put the gun into the trunk of the car.

4   While working for DCAA I did my wash at a laundry across from Monroe Community College. At one time doing my laundry, someone (I believe the Government) put a pink shirt (on purpose) in my wash when I was not looking. The pink ruined all my white clothing. I believe that the Government was trying to discredit me somehow. What do you think?

5   I believe the Government tampered first with the FM radio frequency of my car's FM radio (it died). A week later, the AM frequency on my stereo system died! You can take this as a coincidence but I believe it was **GOVERNMENT HARASSMENT!**

6   In 1991, I was in the RPC Regional Forensic Unit. During my stay, one night, my whole body felt overwhelmingly in pain from three to five minutes in duration. This has never happened to me before. I believe the Government did this. Again, **GOVERNMENT HARASSMENT!** I did have two other incidents; one at St. Mary's and one at home (7-01-02).

7   I developed planter's warts on both my feet. In short, the Podiatrist tried three different remedies (including laser surgery) over a several month period. No remedy worked! Just as soon as I gave up, the planter's warts mysteriously disappeared. I don't know how, I can

only speculate the Government had a part in this; how else did they disappear?

8 I went on a business trip to Detroit with Ken (Coworker). Ken's driver's side window would only roll down half way. Two weeks later my driver's side window would only roll down half way. Do you think this was a coincidence? I believe it was **GOVERNMENT HARASSMENT!**

9 Ben (Manager of DCAA), at a Business Conference, had a warning about Singapore spies. It just so happened I was sharing an apartment with a roommate from Singapore. I told no one, but family, about this roommate. No doubt, I believe DCAA was illegally spying on me (including Ben).

10 **10-12-88:** In my apartment refrigerator I found crystals (white) on wrappings of my chicken. I believe the Government was only showing me who they are (**e.g. First Class Jerks**).

Rochester, NY 2002 – 05:
(A Good Conspiracy Is One That Can't Be Proven)

Because of my **TOP SECRET** work with our **Satanic Government (The Great Satan of America)**, I believe Satan/Government wants me back to work for them; my best guess is for **security** reasons. **I have no inclination to work for these BASTARDS**. Look at the following:

1 I've found scratches and dents on my car. Somebody put them there while I was parked in my back parking lot.

2 Somebody dismantled and stole my car antenna while my car was parked in my back parking lot.

3 Somebody put carved in obscenities on my backyard fence.

4 During this time period, several times, Cops and Fire Cars were parked in the back of my condo. This was harassment to me.

5 I've received phone calls that beep and also calls with no other person on the other end of the phone. Also, other calls with the message saying "message 71".

6 **I've seen several times on cars in front of me on (on various roadways out on the road) their car license plates with G-10, G-11, G-12, G-13, and G-44. I've also seen license plates, many times on the road, from Maryland, Massachusetts, Texas, Colorado, and North Carolina. In retrospect the Government is telling me my so-called future work options (pay grade and areas of work). This is plainly Government Harassment and Oppression.**

7 Since I've worked under **NAVY Top Secret contracts** before, the Government wants me back to work for them – security reasons. **I've**

seen various people flaunt their Old NAVY T-Shirts in front of me mainly in the town of Brockport, NY. I believe this flaunting is and of itself Government instigated. Noted are 2003 dates as follows: 1-04, 1-12, 1-15, 1-18, 2-04, 2-11, 2-19, 2-20, 2-28, 3-03, 3-31, 4-03, 4-08, and 4-16. Also included are 2004 dates as follows: 1-05, 1-21, 2-26, 3-01, 4-19, 4-21, 4-23, 5-18, 5-27, 6-02, 6-07, 6-09, 6-14, 6-18, 6-29, 7-03, 7-05, 7-07, 7-13, 8-17, 9-10, 9-12, 9-26, 9-27, 10-01, 10-04, 10-18, 10-20, 10-24, 11-01, 11-02, 12-19, 12-20. And 2005 dates are as follows: 1-03, 1-04, 1-11, 1-16, 1-26, 2-11, 2-20, 2-22, 2-25, 4-04, 4-25, 5-02, 5-16, 5-22, 6-09, 6-13, 6-20, 6-21, 6-24, 6-27, 6-30, 7-24, 8-19, 9-06, 9-18, 9-25, 10-15, 10-24, 10-27, 11-06, 11-13, 11-19, 12-08, 12-12, 12-25. **I have no ambition to ever work for the Government again.**

8   Parked in my back parking lot next to my car, was a car with **"007"** written on the windshield. I believe this was the work of the Government.

9   One day I was going from my back door to my car out back and a pickup truck almost **ran me over**. I had to jump onto the back of the truck in order to miss getting hit or run over.

CHAPTER 3

FBI, NIS, U.S. Marshall, And NSA
(1986 To Present) — HARASSMENT

Ever since my employment with our Satanic Government, **The Great Satan of America**, (Defense Contract Audit Agency 1987-89) Rochester, NY or also called Field Detachment (1986-1987) Annapolis, MD I believe that the FBI has been **illegally** surveilling me, following me, tapping my phones, and HARASSING me. From this background information you can see some of the Government's **lawbreaking** activities (Noted below is Harassment from the FBI, NIS, U.S. Marshall And NSA). I tried to make a formal complaint against the FBI for its **illegal** surveilling and **HARASSMENT** but with no success. **I would like to know how to get help in a possible civil litigation suit against Hon. John, the FBI, DCAA, and Field Detachment for their illegal activities.**

The following are some impropriety notables in Rochester, New York:

1   **FBI - 8-16-89 1:00 PM** — I called the FBI and spoke to Ted. He would not disclose his last name to me. I told him I gave away classified information to Marta (Therapist & CSW) and gave him her phone number. He said he would check into it. **Ted also asked me for classified information over an uncleared phone line**. This is obviously a breach of security. How could he be so **stupid!**

2   **FBI - 1-17-90 3:15 PM** — Dill (FBI Agent) said he would have James (FBI National Security Specialist) call me back. Dill belligerently and

3   **NIS - 2-01-90 10:00 AM** – Met at my parent's home with a Mr. Valen, (Special Naval Agent Naval Investigative Services – NIS), and he asked me what TOP SECRET INFORMATION I knew of while I worked for the Government. The point here is that he knew my Mom was standing near me when he asked me for the TOP SECRET INFORMATION. My Mom was not cleared to hear any classified information. How **stupid** of him. See **APPENDIX** for FBI/NIS investigation letter results (7-25-90).

4   **FBI – NIS letter dated 25 July 1990** – I highlight the fact that I gave away TOP SECRET classified information. I would have never known that the FBI and the NIS did a **covert** investigation on me if I had not contacted Senator Moynihan and his help. As is in no. 3 above see **APPENDIX** for letter.

5   **FBI – Shortly before 1-07-99** – I was told by my Rochester, NY Public Defender, Mr. Elle, that the FBI was in touch with my Probation Officer asking questions about me. My Probation Officer, Dick, and his Supervisor told me that they could neither confirm nor negate this accusation, which means, to me they did talk to the FBI. The FBI is following me and **HARASSING** me.

6   **FBI** – I wrote a letter dated 13 December 1999 to Congressman John and he had the concern that I would "kill" somebody because I used the word "die" in my letter. Any sixth grader reading the context of this letter or any of my previous letters would know that it doesn't mean that I would "kill" somebody. The reason I wrote this letter was because it was my fifth letter over a period of **seven months** of writing to the Congressman to do a specific investigation of which he never responded to (5-25-99 to 12-13-99). The FBI on **9 May 2000 at 5:30 PM** showed up at my front doorstep and rudely interrupted my dinner. Well, Congressman John thought I might kill somebody because the letter included the word "die". Congressman John told the FBI to investigate me. The FBI received the letter from Congressman John in December 1999. Five months later, the FBI finally showed up at my front doorstep. The FBI compared this letter to the **Oklahoma Bombing of the Federal Building**. If the thought of me killing somebody was thought to be this important (i.e. Why did they wait 5 months to visit or contact me?); then why did the FBI show up at all? I will tell you the reason, it's because the FBI is **HARASSING** me!

7   **U.S. Marshals** – visited me in my apartment and grilled me with all sorts of questions in April 1999. This to me was Government **Harassment.**

8   **FBI 3-24-03 6:45 PM** – At Lowe's (A store) in Greece, NY a person paraded in front of me with an FBI T - Shirt. This is also Government **Harassment.**

9   **NSA (National Security Administration) 1-22-06 & 1-19-06** – Concerning a Northwest Airlines trip from Rochester, NY to Detroit, Michigan (layover) and then to Lexington, KY and back. I believe the NSA was **illegally** following me, trespassing, and harassing me. On 1-22-06 a man had with him take-on luggage which he **overtly** had "**NSA**" written on his luggage in plain sight for me to see at a Detroit, Michigan airplane terminal gate on 1-22-06. This man was flaunting the "**NSA**" in front of me. On 1-19-06 @ Detroit, Michigan Gate B111:20 A.M. a man came to me and said he was from Delaware but worked in Baltimore (I had once lived in Baltimore). Again, on 1-19-06 @ Detroit, Michigan airplane seat A – D Flight terminal on Flight # 3524 a man across from me brought up Baltimore, MD. In summary, I believe the NSA plainly, overtly, and horridly are **illegally** surveilling and following me and harassing me. Talk about against the law. Please, leave me alone!

PALE HORSE OF DEATH

CHAPTER 4

GOVERNMENT PERSECUTION (Field Detachment And DCAA- The Great Satan of America) — My Perspective

Introduction
Body I, II, and III
Conclusion

INTRODUCTION:

The information contained within this article gives you a basic understanding of operations and tells of the criminal acts being performed by our Satanic Government (**The Great Satan of America**). If writing about Satanic criminal acts is considered proprietary/ classified so be it! This testament is an ever present true account of the philosophy and operations of a highly classified sub-organization called Field Detachment which is closely related to the organization known as the Defense Contract Audit Agency (DCAA). Both organizations' mission is to audit Government contracts. These criminal type operations have now filtrated into DCAA (i.e. from the Field Detachment) and I would estimate that 90% of DCAA has incorporated these criminal operations / activities. Presently, it is my contention that these criminal operations are being filtrated to all worldly systems and subsystems originating from the Government.

What does this article try to accomplish? To let the Public know that our Satanic Government is maliciously guilty of forcing employees into demonic possession as follows:

1   The people that work in both these agencies (and all Global Systems/ Subsystems) flagrantly have their **Right of Privacy** denied. Everybody in these systems and subsystems are being spied on at both home and work, and, subject to everywhere. Spying is accomplished by bugging your car, telephones, all rooms in your home and all rooms at your work place. They also watch you through miniature video equipment (surveillance type) of which you are watched in your car, everywhere in your home and at your workplace, and, they even watch you while you take a shower or while you are having sex with your wife. They even know how many times a week you shit. They follow you everywhere you go.

2   The people that work within these agencies are sadistically and unscrupulously **Harassed** everywhere. Depending on an individuals background and the circumstances involved will depict the extent and type of harassment of these lawbreaking hypocrites. Briefly, some main forms of harassment are (a) **No Sleep**-they use a device to render you sleepless, (b) **Noises** – they make constant annoying noises throughout your home, car and even in the work place. As you should know, a combination of no sleep and noises can produce stress which can also lead to a nervous breakdown...the Government has this down to a science!! (c) **Making Work Difficult** – there are many ways to make work difficult, even for the smartest and most intelligent people. If you can think of a way, it is possible. As you

know, this can lead a person to stress as well, and again, possibly a nervous breakdown. (d) **Other** – some other factors such as money situation, car, food, constipation, heartburn, repairs, all come under the domair of harassment/ sabotage (later to be discussed in more detail). A combination of all these...well, there's your Government's science!

3   They **Trespass** relative to both privacy and harassment. The fourth Amendment in the late 1960s was reinterpreted by the Supreme Court in which to provide personal privacy protection. The reinterpretation extended to electronic surveillance coverage which is now covered under the Fourth Amendment. Also, the Omnibus Crime Control act of 1968, which provides certain proscriptions on surveillance by the Court, was enacted whereby an application procedure was mandated to obtain prior approval for electronic surveillance. The Fourth Amendment further states that only with probable cause, appropriate limitations on scope and duration, and prior review are present, invasions of privacy through electronic surveillance techniques are permissible. In both Agencies, none of these criteria are fulfilled. All employees are spied on from day one of being hired into the Agency. Harassment does not start until further down the road when you get more accustomed to the Agency (i.e. approximately 1 – 1.5 years). Since the employees are spied on from day one, it does not fulfill the criteria of "limitation on scope and duration." These people if need be, will falsely make up a story for probable cause so, as a result, the criteria of "probable cause" is not fulfilled. As for the prior review criteria, I'm not sure how this is handled, but, I am sure they will try to get around this criteria somehow. In conclusion, the Government is breaking the law. Why do these people constantly and flagrantly break the law to spy on the employees and harass them? There are three parts to this answer. They are as follows: (a) **Illegally**, they are closely watching the employee so that he/she doesn't leak information (classified) to others, (b) **Illegally**, they are closely watching the employee and their environment so that spies/intruders don't bother you, and, (c) These Hypocrites get a sense of Power, evil that is, over the employees that they are so called ruling over. They abuse the use of their very high tech spying means. Field Detachment is part of that highly sensitive crap just as you see it in the James Bond movies, only, this is the real thing and extremely serious. In this highly classified organization you are just another number whereby security is number one and they could hardly give a damn about the person. This organization will do anything to protect their security and that also means flagrantly violating the law. It was pointed out to me in

this organization, and, I would like for you to pay close attention, think of all possible ways that a person can be spied on and what it is that motivates, depresses, makes happy, sad, or anything else...it has already been thought of by these people. A main point of this book is that over the course of time the Government can blackmail each and every employee in both these Agencies through their sophisticated technology and evil plots and schemes. The Government spends **billions** of dollars to spy. An employee such as myself has spent **zero** dollars trying to defend against such criminal activities going on! I have to emphasize that these people purposefully do **not** leave an **audit trail** in performing criminal/spying activities so that a person such as myself cannot defend against such things. This is why I'm writing this book.

BODY

I. General Sequence of Events In The Organization (The Great Satan of America):

1   When you are first hired you are provided a Special Background Investigation. This investigation goes back 15 years from the present date. This investigation is very detailed and includes trying to get the "skeletons out of your closet" and obtaining any dirty laundry on you that is possible (these are points that are heavily played on in this organization). In other words, they obtain a precise portfolio on you short of reading your mind. There is more to this than what meets the eye.

2   It is noted that before you go into Field Detachment you are only aware that you will be doing auditing type work and that the information you are working with is classified. Who would have ever thought that this organization would spy on, blackmail and harass its own employees. I sure didn't. At least not until well after I joined the damn organization!

3   Assuming you are hired for the job with this organization while the Special Background Investigation is in process (as was my case), you will then be placed in an unclassified area until you are cleared. It will take approximately 6 months to 1 year to be cleared for your security clearances. During your stay in the unclassified areas you basically read the Contract Audit Manual and take a few self-study courses. In other words you don't get much, if any, work experience during this period.

4   Once you have been cleared (i.e. your Special Background Investigation is complete) you will be briefed on a program(s). You are then ready to begin work on these program(s).

5   Times goes on in the Agency, a little over a year, and they slowly get you accustomed to the organization. They start by showing security type films in the work place. The first film provided standard procedures (some) for office security. The second film dealt with spies. In the film the characters (spies) told us that they know how many times a person masturbates and how many times a couple has sex. It was also made plain and clear that these spies can **easily ruin/ destroy** a person's life. During this whole film I thought they were talking about spies going to an adversary country and doing this sort

of thing. I had no idea they were also talking about doing this to their own employees as well!

6   The Agency's next step is to use the information available from the Special Background Investigation (i.e. any skeletons, dirty laundry, or any weakness concerning your background) and start to plot schemes to both blackmail you, and, during the same course of time they will harass you both in and out of your home. When the Government plots & schemes against you, harasses you, and blackmails you it **scares** the hell out of you. This is one reason why nobody ever speaks out against the Government. Also, the Government will do everything in their power to keep this corrupt/criminal activity covert (i.e. from leaking this information). The Government will definitely try to stop an individual if he/she tries to tell of such information. **There is a real possibility of death**.

7   (g) Ultimately you will be blackmailed **into** the organization. A big part of their scheme is to get you leveraged (e.g. in debt). They will encourage you to buy a **new car and own your own home**. This will make it difficult for you to leave any one area quickly in case you wanted to move or get a job elsewhere (because of the harassment and blackmail). If you were thinking about having a lawyer present they will insist that a lawyer not be present and they will tell nothing goes wrong in the **closing** 99.9% of the time. You can even be told that the house won't sell. As I said this is all part of the blackmailing you **into** the organization. They may also try to encourage you to get married. This is to help tie you down...at least at first. If you get married they will start harassing your wife. Most of the time the wife ends up divorcing you. This is why so many people in both organizations are single (one of the main reasons).

8   (h) Once you've been blackmailed and have been in the organization for a substantial period of time (e.g. one of the guys) you may partake (or be forced) in the actual spying of new employees. I estimate as little as three years. The Government involves their employees to spy on new employees because they don't have the resources to hire outside on so many people. As Oliver North would say, "isn't this a great idea!" I say its bull shit! **Note:** The most important point to grasp at this point is that the Government spends Billions of dollars to obtain the most sophisticated/technological equipment and ways and means of spying. So when they plot and scheme and spy, do you think they are going to leave an **audit trail**? If you do, you are crazy!

II. Specific Harassment On The Employees:

Harassment by our Government (Satan) plays a big part of this organization in which **everyone** is subject. Every new employee will be subject to standard harassment procedures. Depending on the employee's background and the circumstances involved there will be a decision on how harsh or involved the harassment should be. If you are a stubborn employee, as myself, you will be given full treatment... a nervous breakdown. If you are a poor innocent girl that is afraid of everything, she will most likely just receive standard treatment. In my case they gave me a nervous breakdown. As you should know, our Satanic Government (**The Great Satan of America**) **precalculated** what it would take to give me a nervous breakdown (oh how I would like to put them in jail for this).

The reason for harassment is to scare the hell out of you and if you don't **Condescend** to these people they will keep on harassing you. Of course, these people will **not** leave an **audit trail** when they harass you (a conspiracy).

Again, spying is a big part to harassment. If you have been in the organization for approximately three years you may take part in the actual spying on the new employees. You may also be forced to spy even if it is against your will to do so. When the employee is not in his/her car and out of the office and/or home there are several ways they can still pick up his/her conversation. One way is to have a dentist put a bug in the filling of your tooth and another is to use some sort of sensing device from a distance to pick up your voice /conversation. There are several ways. During my main period of harassment, almost every time I went to the office there would be at least one other staff person present (I was never left alone). Also, each and every day there would be missing one staff person (e.g. each day a different person). The missing staff person was designated to spy on me both in the office and out. Spying on you by a designated office person is as follows: (1) records telephone conversations and (2) use some sort of homing device to follow you.

Satan's system involves Government **Oppression** whereby you are forced into a system of being demonically possessed (a heavily guarded system). It's my belief that a ritual is performed whereby you dress up in a black robe & hood, chant, & become possessed as part of the system. My college fraternity had such a ritual. They had fraternity brothers dress in black robes and chanted "Hail to the Garnet and Gold". **The following are specific examples of Government Oppression which leads to "demonic-possession":**

A. *Various:*

Our Satanic Government oppresses you or forces you to the point of submission to the demonic system. The Government can force the following on you: diarrhea, constipation (until recently I've never had this), double chin, obesity, allergies, brittle or fungus of the finger or toe nails (my mother had to surgically take toe nails off), warts (happened to me once), poor eye vision (blindness – a family member is blind, cataracts, ect.), dry skin (I have dry skin even though I'm no longer a swimmer), bad calluses, back aches, acne, non controllable bowel movements (happened to me once), arthritis, coughing (at one time I was uncontrollably coughing for six months straight), seizures (my cousin had these), gout (step dad had this), blackouts (my cousin and sister had these), Alzheimer's disease, colitis (step dad and my coworker had this), crohns disease (girlfriend had this), acid indigestion (several family members), kidney stones (several family members, my pastor, & my cousin's husband), appendix out (three family members), nausea (cousin had this), joint replacements (family members), athletes foot (myself), jock itch (myself), acid reflux disease (my dad an sister), home infestations, herpes, ears ringing (sister in law), and loss of hearing (my mother and Rush Limbaugh). And many more not mentioned.

B. *Death:*

Satan's system's last resort to get rid of a noncompliant antisystematic person is to underhandedly put them to death. Per Government Oppression you can get **Cancer** (lives lost to High School Teachers-Social Studies, Math, Biology, and English (a brain aneurysm)), stomach, brain tumor, uterus, ovary, prostate, adhesions (my sister has), breast, colon, etc.. Some other means by which the Government can put you to death are heart attack, stroke, diabetes, cholesterol, bubonic plague, fry born disease, SARS, mad cow disease, west nile virus, and lime disease. The Government can even get you into a fatal car accident (a lady in our church died in a car accident and another close friend; I've been in two car crash totals). Other fatalities include liver disease, kidney failure, epilepsy, multiple sclerosis, lupus, pneumonia, and aides. I remember a Junior High School student who shot his head off and recently a church family father shot himself to death **(these days there are record people who commit suicide, children and adult).** Again, you either comply to both becoming demonically-possessed and part of the system or your final destination is death!

C. Labeled As Gay Or Homophobic:

Satan and or the Government will try to discredit you by labeling you or any possibility of anyone as gay or homophobic. People who have been labeled as gay are Prince Charles, Jim Baker (evangelist), Tom Cruise, Oprah Winfrey, remember the U.S.S. Iowa sailor, and I've heard of Jesus Christ as being Homophobic. For your information there are many demon-possessed homosexuals/lesbians. A few noted; Elton John, Ellen, and Rosie.

D. Sleep (Main Form of Harassment):

The Government has a device which can render you sleepless. The device will interfere with your REM sleeping patterns. In other words you will not be able to sleep. The device is used on everybody in the organization and is one of their main means of harassment. How do I know of such a device? Well, the Government purposefully lets you know by **projecting a commercial on your television set portraying a Government official with a teenager (who discovered such a device) and the Government wants to buy out the rights to it.** It is noted that this means of communication is a part of how the Government communicates to its employees **without** leaving an **audit trail**. As Oliver North would say, "isn't this a great idea!" The two ways which this device works and forces you into Satan's system is as follows:

1. **Steady Stream** – the device is run constantly therefore you cannot sleep at any time while the device is running.
2. **Blips** – the device will turn on periodically but only before each and every time you're almost asleep. It is analogous to a current of electricity hitting you just before you fall asleep.

Note:

If you are seeing a psychiatrist then you may have an EEG test performed on you (e.g. a test of brain wave patterns). During the actual testing, the sleepless device can be turned on in the Blip mode and alter your brain wave patterns. In other words, these people can tamper with the results of the test whereby they have false evidence of saying that your brain waves are screwed up. They can also alter truth detection tests the same way.

I described how the Government sleeping devices can keep you awake at night. What I want to tell you is that they can also do just the opposite; they can also make you very sleepy. They can put you out like a light. For example, do you recall President Ronald Reagan falling asleep during meetings? Also, Vice President Dick Cheney as well?

E. Car:

There are any number of things that the system can do to your car. The way this scenario works, the people at your work place pretend to get on the phone with his/her car dealer and he/she will say that their passenger window doesn't roll up or down properly (it's broken). Then what happens is in a short time your **own** passenger car window just happens to not roll up or down properly. This method is to let you know that the Government (Satan) means business and you have to condescend to them. As noted, this is another method of communication/harassment that leaves no **audit trail**.

Some other things they do to your car are as follows:

1   They may increase the mileage (the odometer reading) very quickly so as to have a basis/reason to sabotage your car (i.e. for harassment purposes). If you, the reader, has an open mind then you can see that the more the mileage on a car, the more likely something can go wrong with it. Right!

2   They can place nails in your tire(s) or adjust the nozzle for a slow air leak.

3   They may put a different type of tire on your car, one that is worn down in several places making a thumping sound. This noise can be very annoying along with your heater or air conditioner.

4   They can put worn down window wipers on your car.

5   They can make your engine stop any number of ways and any number of times.

6   They can break your radio. They may disconnect FM or AM or both.

7   They can put a device on your gears so that when you park the car and put it in gear to keep the car from rolling they will activate the device and your car will start rolling.

8   They can project any music, commercial, their own broadcast, or whatever fits their purpose over your radio. This is a method used to communicate to you for their purposes. For example, lets say that the Government has been keeping you awake for several nights (by a Government's sleepless device) and you have a clock radio alarm where you wake to a music alarm; well, to further harass you, you will awake the next morning with the lyrics that goes something like, **"Why can't you sleep at night?"** Like I say, this is just one example. These people are just a bunch of bastards!

F. Noises In The Home (Another Main Form of Harassment):

Noises play a big part in harassment. When the Government puts electronic or other types of noises throughout your home this is also a way to let you know that they mean business and that they are spying on you.

The Government is clever in that they will pick a noise(s) to harass you that sounds like the environment around you (i. e. crickets, water heater pipes, faucets dripping, etc). This is another way that the Government gets around leaving an **audit trail.** When they really want to harass you they will increase the frequency of the sound or increase the loudness or they can shift the sound to a different point in a room. Just another means to compliance to Satan's system.

1   **Crickets** – The Government uses micro electronic devices which make cricket noises. I've tried looking for these devices when they have spied on me but I have failed. In fact, my Supervisor told me not to bother looking for these micro type devices because I will never find them. The Government does not have to just use cricket noises, they can use any noise their heart desires (i.e. birds chirping, locust noises, water heater pipe noises are a very big item, and **mice** running in your ceiling and walls is a **very big item**).

2   **Refrigerator** – The Government can make the motor on the back of the refrigerator loose so that any annoying clamoring type sound is made.

3   **Water Faucets** – The Government can make the faucets drip to make an annoying dripping sound.

4   **Toilet** – The Government can easily adjust the mechanism that fills the water tank so that the water keeps running and makes an annoying sound.

G. Food:

This is also a scenario which involves the people in the work place. The Government tries to play games with your mind. The people in your office will say that the food I eat at lunchtime is too greasy (i. e. high cholesterol). They will tell you **not** to use the same plate you used to place the raw chicken on after you're done cooking it. They will go on and on about these types of things until you literally think you have to buy the best brand name foods and cook them perfectly. Also, of course, you should wash your dishes immediately after dinner otherwise you may pick up some sort of disease, so the people in the office indicate. In other words, you have to do these things perfect or the Government would possibly have a basis to put an actual germ on your plate or food. They have now told you their basis for such things. Again, there is no audit trail if they decide to transmit some sort of germ to you if you do not meet their standards. If you even mention that your food cholesterol intake is above normal they have a basis to give you a mild heart attack (in other words, you are being blackmailed into the system and if you go against that system they would have a basis to suddenly dispose of your ass). Again, comply with Satan's system?

H. Colds:

The Government can put cold germs into the air (by means of a mixture of cold germs and dust particles) both through the heating and air conditioning units of your home and car. Also these people can easily put cold germs on a cup that you frequently drink out of, with ease. Again, comply with Satan's system?

I. Teeth:

Another way to harass you is to give you bad teeth. From the water, floss, or mouthwash there are a number of ways to get bad teeth. In my case the Dental Hygienist wore away my tooth enamel near the tooth gum line during the cleanings. What the Government's interest is to try to either give you a root canal or pull one of your teeth. Why? They can put some kind of microelectronic device in your roots so that they can activate this device from a distance and hurt your tender roots with electrical impulses. They would do this not only to harass but to blackmail you as well. Or possibly place in your roots some sort of homing device or bug or combination. This is why I say that they must want to do something different when they go for a root canal or pulling of a tooth in which the sensitive roots are involved. While in **Maryland**, my dentist wanted to fix five cavities and take out all wisdom teeth. Returning to **New York**, my dentist did not recommend nearly as much. This is just another way to be forced to do the Government's bidding.

J. Payroll & Travel Reimbursement:

This is another form of harassment to keep you on your toes. You have to keep a close watch on whether you get reimbursed for these. I've actually had to call payroll before and tell them to pay me because of non-receipt of payment. They play the same types of games with travel reimbursement (they purposefully postpone reimbursement to harass). Again, comply with Satan's system?

K. Entering Your Home:

Entering your home is no problem to these people. After all, they are in the business of spying. They monitor your home at all times so they know who is home or not. One of their more challenging feats, as was told by to me by one of the employees in the office, is to sneak into your home at night while you are asleep and do what they please. Oh, the Government will let you know of such things by means of charades in the office. Charades will be explained in more detail later. Again, comply with Satan's system?

L. Hair Loss:

Another big form of harassment is that of hair loss. The Government can easily sneak into your home and put a hairloss substance either in the water or shampoo itself. You will notice substantial, but gradual hair loss over time. I have noticed that this form of harassment was used on my Supervisor during a more intense period of my harassment. They were trying to force my Supervisor to do certain improprieties in connection with me (i.e. non-promotion, certain bad reviews, and just being hard-nosed). They were doing this sort of thing so I would have incentive to move elsewhere; to a different job and area. At one point my Supervisor was practically bald. But after she did what they wanted, her hair grew back. They pulled this hair loss stunt on me in Maryland (for harassment purposes). Again, comply with Satan's system?

III. Blackmail And Operations of Organization:

One way to blackmail you from giving out classified information or any information of the corrupt practices of the Government (Satan's System) is through harassment and threat of death. Harassment scares a person and the Government can harass at any time and in any duration they see fit.

A. Intercepting Phone Calls:
By listening to your phone conversations (both at home and at work) over a substantial period of time the Government knows who all your phone calls are. If you get on the phone and dial the phone number of someone, they know immediately the phone number and who is possibly on the other end. These people have on file all your phone contacts voice patterns for their immediate use. In other words, once you dial the phone number they know all the people that are at the other end of the line. The Government will immediately intercept the phone call by having one of their people talk with you (an imposter) but sounding exactly like the person you want to talk with (it could be anyone in your family, business contacts, or any other contact). It is also noted that the Government (DCAA) has you complete every two weeks a two week projection report (i.e. that is when you're actually working on the job). This tells them of any future sick leave or annual leave (vacation) that you may be taking for the next two weeks. It gives them time to scope any situation /appointment that may be at hand. What happens is you first have to make an appointment with the dentists or doctors office. The Government could intercept your phone call (an imposter) and ask for an appointment. What possibility the Government can do is set you up with a corrupt/ crooked dentist (anyone). They can bribe this dentist/doctor to perform a service for the Government on you (anything). To remember, they monitor all your phone calls. **As such, I'm only implying this as one of several possibilities.**

B. Impostors:
This is a very clever tool and is easily accomplished in this business. To be an impostor you need to look exactly like the person you are impersonating, you need to have the same voice pattern, and you need to have some general knowledge of that person. I'm not sure, but they somehow use a device to make the impostor's voice pattern match the person being impersonated. It should be carefully noted that the Government can impersonate you yourself. This, in itself, is a big part of **blackmailing** you. What they can do is have someone that looks exactly like you and has the

same voice pattern, and, video tape this imposter in bed (having sex) with as many girls or guys as dictated. As you recall, **Saddam Hussien** (of Iraq), Saddam's videotapes were recovered by the U.S.Government and had to seek its authenticity (also, the U.S. can easily make an (un) authenic tape also on anyone as well).

C. Getting Out of The Organization:

If you send resumes out they can intercept your mail and send you back standard company letterheads stating rejection. Unless you personally know the person hiring you, you can forget getting a job elsewhere. To them, you are married to the job, some exceptions noted.

D. Charades:

Charades is also a big part in this organization. It's a part of harassment, a part of blackmail, a way to let you know they are spying on you, and eventually a way to show you that you must play a condescending role. What is involved is yourself and the staff at your workplace. The charade is accomplished by having the staff plot & scheme a scenario in which they can try one of two things (1) make you apart of the scenario or (2) not make you apart of the scenario but want you to hear it.

One thing you have to keep in mind about this is that what I'm about to tell you was preplanned by the office. When we got back from a business trip, Will (an auditor) kept saying that our trip included **debauchery** and said that we had the **wildest** time. An auditor emphasized the words "**debauchery**" and "**wildest**" over and over to an extreme. He also brought up the word "**Hogans**". This word represents a lady's chest. From that time on he started to call me "**Hogans**".

Another auditor in our office was next directed by the Government to play up big on calling me "Hogans". For the next several weeks this auditor called me **Hogans** and kept telling the staff all about the debauchery and wild times in Detroit. This whole thing was a ploy to discredit myself (if need be). I have to say that we did not have a so-called wild time nor was debauchery a part of this. We had a good time and a couple of drinks. I finally resented the staff calling me Hogans, so they stopped. The point of all this is that the Government has this on video tape and the conversation recorded of which they would use to **blackmail** me.

Another example of number one (1) above is that the office staff will try to get you to say bad or nasty things about the organization as a whole, about a specific employee, or about the work itself. How this works is that one staff member of the office will be designated as the instigator. This person will ahead of time prepare a scheme or scenario of which to use on me (the new employee) and set me up. They will use this scheme or scenario to leave me **wide-open** to say such bad or nasty things. Again, this is all on video and recorded conversation and is used to blackmail me. I can recall three instances where an auditor tried these schemes on me but I had already caught on before I said some of these nasty things.

Some examples for number two (2) above are as follows: When I was in Maryland, the office staff would repeat a word or phrase in our office **(the very next day)** of which I had said this word or phrase the very night **before** in my apartment (I tested this twice with two different phrases). Again, the Government wanted me to know that I was being spied on and that I should condescend to them. Over a period of time I finally caught on. Again, as I have previously stated earlier, I decided to test my theory that they were spying on me. As stated earlier before, they were in fact **illegally** spying on me.

Another example involves another employee. The DCAA Manager **(Ben)** came into our office one day and had a suit jacket on that was un-stitched almost all the way around one of his shoulders. He told us that he knew of this but he still wanted to wear this jacket. He also told us that he had worn this previously and didn't mind wearing it. My point is that an authoritative person doesn't **knowingly** wear a suit jacket in which the whole shoulder area is unstitched. Especially if he has other suits to wear. My next point is that a month later my suit jacket was also unstitched. To spell this out, the Government broke the law and came into my home and unstitched my suit jacket.

E. Non-Promotion:

These people (the Government) were trying to move me. Chad (cowork-er) told me the Government wanted to send me to Saudi Arabia – **Underhandedly and Wantonly by Government Oppression**, some people within the system kept bringing the Saudi Arabia idea up to me. First of all, I hate Saudi Arabia! I have no ambition to leave Rochester, New York, at all, under **any circumstances**!

The way they were trying to accomplish this **(by force)** was by the following:

1 **Not promoting me** – they were trying to entice me to go elsewhere.
2 **Getting along with the office** – the people in the office will specifically be directed not to get along with me especially my Supervisor. My Supervisor is the one who directly supervises me and is the one with whom I have the greatest need to get along with...especially if I want a promotion.
3 Once they accomplish these two tasks they will specifically ask me if I want to move or work out of the Buffalo office. If I did accept, then

they would eventually make up some other reasons to move me from the Buffalo office (**to some other distant place**). Then they could harass me al they want (they want my total condescension).

Conclusion:

As shown, the Government is flagrantly violating the law. They, in effect, are forcing Government employees to worship them. The Government is invading employees privacy, forcing employees to do things against their will, and not least, they are tormenting/torturing the employees ... especially if they do not condescend or abdicate.

CHAPTER 5

Incompetencies And Improprieties
Arrests, Judges, Jail, & Attorneys
Another Great Satan System

Arrested 9-13-90 Arraignment Greece Town Court — Judge Barron:
On 9-13-90 I was arrested and arraigned for breaking a front and rear windshield of a brand new car at a car dealership.

The following are incompetencies and improprieties at Arraignment:

1   The Greece police / escort service put me in leg cuffs and handcuffs at the court Arraignment on 9-13- 90. **While in court, they took my prescription eyeglasses off in which I could not see properly (including the Judge Barron). I pleaded with Judge Barron to put my eyeglasses on to see him and the courtroom properly. Judge Barron only stared at me like a retard.** I believe I have the right to properly see Judge Barron and the whole court room processes. Judge Barron sat on his but and did nothing; Why? Is Judge Barron competent to make reasoned decisions concerning others or me? I believe not!

2   Through inquiry with Judge Barron he plainly said, "I had no right to the presence of an attorney"; without any qualification to this statement. He purposely tried to confuse this matter.

3   Judge Barron told me I was being given $1,000 bail. This to me was excessive bail because this was my **first offense**.

4   Judge Barron **read the wrong crime** for myself. I did not break a window; I broke the front and rear windshields of a new car at a car dealership. Is Judge Barron competent?

5   The Greece Police stoled my set of keys on 9-13-90 with the exception of my car keys.

Monroe County Jail Abuses (1990) includes writings- Superintendent of this jail dated 11-12 & 11-26-91:

1   On the evening of September 14, 1990 I was called into the Monroe County Jail office (the smaller office), at Main Control, to answer their medical background questions in the presence of 4 to 5 Deputies. I was sitting down in a chair just trying to mind my own business. When the Deputy asked me to answer their medical background questions I told him I'm exercising my legal right not to answer these questions and that I wanted to see my lawyer before I answer **any** questions. Of course, this was not good enough for these Deputies. As I was sitting down, the Deputies (3 of them), would "**scream**" in my face the words "**Fucked Up**" by saying, **"Why Are You So FUCKED UP?"** in my face. I told them repeatedly that I'm exercising my right **not** to answer their medical background questions. The Deputies screamed repeatedly this obscene phrase in my face 5 to 6 times and I repeatedly responded by saying my **"rights"** 5 to 6 times over and over. Let me just say, if you had several people (Deputies) scream in your face, especially an obscenity, it would have an adverse effect on you and may forcibly make you answer their medical background questions (**as I did not**); I held on to my rights and beliefs. These Deputies were **BARBARIC**! They also told me repeatedly that I was **not cooperating** by not answering their medical background questions and telling me I will be in jail a lot longer if I did not answer these questions. For your knowledge, I have the legal right **not** to so call **"COOPERATE"**. Plain and simple, I don't have to answer their stupid questions. Who gave these God Forsaken Deputies the right to exercise such **BARBARIC** and unlawful tactics? First, these tactics try to **forcibly** make me answer their medical background questions; it's no wonder this is unlawful. And Second, I was significantly harassed.

2   In my possession, I had a sheet of paper that was given to me from Judge Barron. It had information concerning future court dates, who my Public Defender would be, etc.. This sheet of paper was taken by one of the Deputies and crumpled it and threw it into the wastebasket. He did this with **no** reason and I never got the sheet back. By the way, my mother, a couple of weeks ago, went to the Monroe

County Jail with a sheet of paper concerning my personal property (she only wanted to pick up my personal items) and the Deputy took this sheet of paper from her and ripped it up. She was harassed! I think Superintendent's jail is run by a system off thugs (Satan himself). Here again the jail system is another Satanic system; one of Global systems.

3   On the evening of October 26, 1990 a Corporal called me back into the same office as described above. This Corporal closed the door so nobody could see what he was about to do. Can you believe that a Corporal would do such a thing? The Corporal wanted me to sign a form so I would get my deposited cash out of the Monroe County Sheriff's account. I would not sign because there was a discrepancy in amount. The Corporal said I could not resolve the discrepancy that day because the computer was down but he wanted me to sign anyway. I did not sign because I only wanted to sign when I could resolve the discrepancy. **The Corporal got mad at me and took both his hands and hit me on my chest** (I remind you I was sitting and sitting placidly). I feel this to be harassment and assault. **Who in the HELL gave him the right to hit me?** As the system dictates, he did this behind closed doors, with no fault of mine!

4   On the following dates, (9-13-90 to 9-18-90), (10-16-90 to 10-26-90), and (12-08-90 to 12-11-90), I was in jail with no towel issued to me. The Deputies wanted me to dry off from a shower with a pillowcase. **HOW BARBARIC!** So I just did not take a shower; the longest period being 10 days. **Also, while in jail, I went two days without drink because the Deputies would not give me a cup (i.e. part of Satan's Globalwide System).**

5   On (9-13-90 to 9-18-90) and (12-08-90 to 12-11-90), **subsequent to my arrests**, I was denied my **one free** phone call while in prison on these dates. And during the week of (12-08-90 to 12-11-90) I asked if I could get my one free phone call. **Corporal Santone** escorted me into his office. He asked me if I wanted to answer medical background questions. I said no because I'm exercising my legal rights not to answer these questions. He said if I answer the medical questions I would be allowed several phone calls from his office. I asked if I could get my one free phone call without answering the medical background questions and **Corporal Santone** said no. This is blackmail and a denied right to one free phone call subsequent to arrest. Because I would not answer any of these questions, **Corporal Santone** was very nasty to me (i.e. swearing, etc.). Who put this thug in charge? Just part of Satan's System.

By Mark C. Russell

6   During the dates described above, I was denied the right to go to a church service. Because of this, **I wrote several Written Grievances** to let me go to a church service, which in their own Policies and Procedures I have the right to practice such freedom of religion. They plainly denied me such right which also included no responses to my Written Grievances. Stated, they should have responded accordingly within their Policies and Procedures. I received no response. Again, Satan is working overtime!

Arrested & Arraigned On 12-08-90 Clarkson
Justice Town Court – Judge Pograe:
On 12-08-90 I was arrested for burning a shed in the town of Parma. Why if from Parma was I in a Clarkson Town Court? The following are incompetencies an improprieties at Arraignment:

1   Judge Pograe (presided), myself, a Monroe County policeman, and two fire department people were present. I had asked what was the purpose of the proceeding. Judge Pograe said this was a **Preliminary Hearing**. I later asked him again; he then said this was an **Arraignment**. I think this older gentleman purposefully is losing his memory (Satan at work).
2   The Monroe County police would **not** let me attain a lawyer.
3   The Arraignment, I thought, is usually where charges are formally presented, rights read, and a pleading; charges or rights were not formally presented. I don't understand why the fire department had my Accusatory Instrument (Felony Arson Charges) in their possession. The fire department (in the courtroom) put or stuffed my felony charges in my pocket. Should not the Judge have had it in his possession while the court proceeding was in session and then he submit it to me? **Why did the Accusatory Instrument not have the Judge's name or signature on it?** This is an Internal Control Procedure weakness (Satan's System)!
4   The Monroe County police on the way to the local jail took me to the crime scene in Parma. I told the Policeman I did not want to go to the crime scene and he said, "to bad".
5   I asked Judge Pograe for the copy of next court date reminder sheet. He said he had no copy to give me but to get one from the Monroe County police officer at the Monroe County jail. I had asked for this notice but simply I never received one; ever!
6   Judge Pograe set no bail and I asked why. He said it was the District Attorney's recommendation. If I had my own Attorney, I would have

had "no bail" charge recommended to "bail" or "out on my own recognizance". This, to me, violates my Constitutional Rights.

Ms. Bell (My Assistant Public Defender) For Arrests On (9-13-90) & (12-08-90):

1 To date (i.e. relative to arrest on 9-13-90) I have never received an Accusatory Instrument Form stating charges against me from either the Court cr my Public Defender Ms. Bell. I was never made aware of such a form nor did Ms. Bell and the Court make me aware that I have the legal right to inspect such documentation before going to court.

2 I asked Ms. Bell what was my reduction of charges for the broken windshields case. Ms. Bell told me that the District Attorney was going to accept a reduction of charges for a plea of Guilty to Criminal Mischief 3rd to Criminal Mischief 5th degree. There is no such thing as a Criminal Mischief 5th degree; the lowest being fourth degree. Ms. Bell's excuse for not knowing the correct Criminal Mischief degree was that she does not do many Misdemeanors. I believe this to be a poor excuse for a person who has passed the bar exam. Also, Ms. Bell says she mainly deals with Felonies. So then, my question is, "Doesn't an Attorney try to reduce Felonies to Misdemeanors?" And is Ms. Bell competent to make reasoned decisions concerning my behalf? I know not!

3 At the jail, told Ms. Bell that I had money in my Savings/Checking account to cover the $1,000 bail (Set by Judge Barron on 9-13-90) for this crime. I told Ms. Bell that I had nobody who could bail me out and did not know of a way to get my money out of my account. Ms. Bell said other than Jail Ministries she did not know how to get me out on bail. As such, she did not even mention the concept of a bail bondsperson as well. Ms. Bell's reason for not knowing; she told me it's a learning experience for both of us. I rotted in jail for 10 days (i.e. 10-16-90 to 10-26-90) waiting for Ms. Bell to figure it out. Again, is Ms. Bell competent to make reasoned decisions concerning my behalf? I krow not!

4 I asked Ms. Bell (well before Christmas) about how to go about paying restitution. Per Criminal Mischief Law Section 420.10 there are three ways to pay Restitution. Ms. Bell mentioned two out of the three whereby failing to mention number three. Ms. Bell never gave me complete written or oral instructions on how to pay Restitution. I may have used number three of the mentioned code if brought to

my attention. I believe Ms. Bell to be incompetent as to making reasoned decisions concerning myself.

5   I was arrested on **9-13-90** and was put in the Monroe County Jail on bail until **9-18-90.** I believe I was put at Rochester Psychiatric Center (RPC) Forensic Unit **falsely** from (**9-18-90 to 10-16-90**) and subsequently put in jail from **10-16-90 to 10-26-90** until released from jail (on my own recognizance)on **10-26-90; Why so long?** On **9-13-90** bail was set at $1,000 by Judge Barron and I could have been out of jail shortly thereafter if I had knowledge of access to my money but **I was denied the right to the presence of an Attorney** on **9-13-90** by Judge Barron and never saw an Attorney (i.e. Ms. Bell – Assistant Public Defender) until after several days of being at RPC Forensic Unit. On **10-16-90 I proved in Court** that the Forensic Unit held no cognizance as to Involuntary Care And Treatment. I was not Hospitalized at all while at the Forensic Unit and basically sat and minded my own business. I wanted to sue for False Imprisonment but Ms. Bell said no. Again, I could have been out of jail on $1,000 bail on **9-13-90.** Again, is Ms. Bell competent to make reasoned decisions concerning my behalf? I know not!

6   On **12-24-90** I told Ms. Bell that in the newspaper the other day a Webster, NY Businessman and an Attorney were both brought up on charges of **laundering $300,000 of Drug Trafficking Money and the Attorney got out on his own recognizance.** Myself, on the other hand, only broke a front and rear windshield of a car that costs just hundreds of dollars. **My bail was set at $1000 by Judge Barron. Compare $300,000 of Laundering Drug Trafficking Money to my hundreds of dollars of broken windshields and that before this charge I had a perfectly clean record and was an outstanding member of the community**; I believe this to be **excessive bail** in my case. I told Ms. Bell I wanted to sue under my Constitutional Rights (i.e. excessive *bail & grievance*) and Ms. Bell said no. Do you think the Government (i.e Satan's system) had a part in this? I know so!

7   I told Ms. Bell on **12-24-90** that on 12-08-90, to date, I was denied a free phone call at both the Monroe County Jail and RPC Forensic Unit. Ms. Bell's response was negative and said to me there is no statute or Constitution that says I'm entitled to one free phone call subsequent to arrest and that I can not sue for its denial. I, however, beg to differ.

Mr. Conn (Mental Hygiene Legal Service – MHLS (Attorney)) 1991-1993:

Mr. Conn (12-22-90):

Mr. Conn said I'm on a combination of 508 Correction Law and Mental Hygiene Law 9.37. Mr. Conn said 508 Correction Law is where the Judge issues a court order to have an exam done and get me at the Forensic Unit and the Mental Hygiene Law is where the psychiatrist/physician determines involuntary status or not. Mr. Conn said Form OMH 461A (4-78) was **incorrect** – Notice of Status And Rights – Conversion – To Involuntary Status. This Form had wrongly preprinted information (i.e. Section 9.13 (b). M.H. Law). This particular section means **voluntary**. **Never** in a million years did I volunteer to be at the Forensic Unit; quite the contrary. The Form should have read Mental Hygiene Law 9.27 – Two Doctor's Signatures. This was one of many improprieties.

Mr. Conn (1-10-91 & 1-11-91):

I was told from Mr. Conn that I was on a combination of 508 Correctional Law & M.H.Law 9.27. Per 508 Correction Law the Director of the State Hospital files the application supported by the Certificate of two physicians. I was told by Mr. Conn and Deputy Dunn there are no Forms telling a patient that they are on or fall under the jurisdiction of Correction Law 508 and the way you find out is through your lawyer. This is a weakness in Internal Contro ; there is no paper audit trail and I believe a patient, like all other admissions, should receive in writing the 508 Status. Under 508 Correction Law it says admission and retention fall pursuant to Sections 31.37 or 31.39 and 31.27, 31.37or 31.39. Why no Forms telling me as such? Also, per Rights of Inpatients... in psychiatric centers of the NYS OMH Handbook page 6 it says, "Upon admissions you will receive a notice about your admission status..." Where was my so called 508 Correction Law Notice (i.e. written) upon Forensic Unit admission?

Mr. Conn (1-11-91):

Per Forensic Unit Handbook Page 14 under "Social Worker " it says, "The information obtained by the Social Worker in these areas is very important in aiding the psychiatrist in determining your mental condition." Point being, if you want to make one legal phone call (or more) to obtain a lawyer of my choice I need to contact a Social Worker and have her escort and Supervise me. Mr. Conn, after consulting with his peers, thought it unreasonable that I make a phone call in which to secure an attorney of my choice on the usual Wednesdays and Fridays mornings where we are allowed to make one "legal" phone call each day. We are only allowed to call an Attorney **on record** on Wednesdays and Fridays. Plainly, I did not want any connection with a Social Worker and subsequently have this Social Worker trump up any adverse information directed to the psychiatrist /whomever. Policy does not state other than we are allowed to make "legal" phone calls. I would think that if I provided a name and number of a potential Attorney, this would be considered a "legal " phone call and reasonable for the usual Wednesday and Friday "legal" phone calls which are supervised by an Aide rather than a Social Worker (page 5 of the Patient Handbook states this difference). As before, policy is dictated at will.

Mr. Conn (2-04-91):

In a letter dated 16 December 1990 to a Mr. Conn (Mental Hygiene Legal Service (MHLS) –Attorney) I had asked or requested, "I strongly request that I obtain written notification of the purpose (why?) of my placement at RPC (Forensic Unit) by both psychiatrists and surrounding reasons (basis), if any." Upon our meeting, Mr. Conn's reason why I did not receive anymore information was because "this is all that Mr. Conn had in his possession." Well, I requested this information on 16 December 1990 and it's now 4 February 1991. My court date for MHLS to get me a discharge/release from the Forensic Unit is tomorrow (5 February 1991). How are we supposed to prepare for a court case under these circumstances (i.e. lack of vital information)? Where is my lawyer – incompetence? Why does he not inform me of what is going on even after requesting such information in writing and in person?

Mr. Conn (3-15-91):

The time was approximately 4:20 – 4:45 PM; I had met with Mr. Conn. I had originally asked Mr. Cent (Chief of Service of Forensic Unit) on both (1-11-91) and (1-26-91) for my use of the Mental Hygiene Law. Mr. Cent never got back to me. Per Mr. Conn (MHLS Attorney), he asked his Supervisor about getting the Mental Hygiene Law to me and his **Supervisor said, 'all patients are not allowed to borrow or have access to the Mental Hygiene, Corrections, or Criminal Procedure Laws'.** I pointedly stated that the Forensic Unit Facility does not have access to these Laws as well. Therefore, everyone is not allowed access to these Laws to which I believe violates our basic Rights and violates the Law flagrantly. I believe this is to be against our Constitutional Rights; don't you?

CHAPTER 6

Incompetencies And Improprieties
Rochester Psychiatric Center (RPC) Regional
Forensic Unit (1990 – 1993)
Another Great Satan System

INTRODUCTION:

I was admitted to **The Rochester Psychiatric Center (RPC) Regional Forensic Unit** (12/90 – 1993) in a Satanistic System that's in and of itself; one of many regional and global systems. This unit takes in many helpless people in a system that is manipulative to make these people appear to be psychotic, mentally ill, and a danger. In my case, Dr. Zin, Psychiatrist (and several others in the Forensic Unit) did everything they could do to make me out as mentally ill and a danger to myself or others. This was done because the Government wants me to look psychotic in a Top Secret Environment. I will challenge anybody as to the allegations brought up by anybody specifically, Dr. Zin and Dr. Sing. The following pages reflect the people that were involved with my stay at The RPC Regional Forensic Unit and how they all participated in each of their roles in one of many regional and Global Satanic Systems. This is a continuation of Satan's System involving improprieties of such a system!

Dr. Zin M.D. (Forensic Unit Psychiatrist 1990 - 1991):

12-20-90:

I have the right to **not** talk to Dr. Zin. Dr. Zin just kept pressing me to answer and discuss personal family matters. I had repeatedly told him not to bring up these matters especially with his relentless pursuit; it was plain **harassment.**

12-21-90:

Dr. Zin interrupted my lunch to again ask me several personal questions; again, I plainly did not want to answer his personal questions. This was harassment.

1-14-91:

Dr. Zin **again** wanted to discuss facts / opinions relative to family/relatives problems related to me. I did, and needed to tell him to plainly to **"shut up"**; again, plainly it's my right not to answer or discuss any of his questions. This was harassment.

1-16-91:

I asked Dr. Zin when the court hearing will be for medication of 60-day retention and/or end of 60 days court hearing to keep me six more months. **He replied that he did not know how the system works.** What an idiot!

1-25-91:

Dr. Zin said I had to get my own lawyer for the court hearing. I found out contrary to his statement; I can request that a member of the hospital staff contact for me the Mental Hygiene Legal Services. What a jerk!

1-29-91:

I needed a letter to be written by Dr. Zin to get me out of my apartment lease. After much discussion with Dr. Zin he ended up saying, "I don't care about your apartment lease", and then he left me.

2-01-91:

Dr. Zin came into the day room for the first time to sit and observe. Very rarely did Dr. Zin sit and observe. How can he make any valid conclusions or opinions concerning me (without first hand observation) and is Dr. Zin competent to make any reasoned judgements concerning myself? I know not!

2-05-91:
Dr. Zin again, relentlessly, tried to ask me personal questions. I again, plainly said no to talking with him. This was harassment.

4-06-91:
For my second criminal offense of which I was arrested for, Dr. Zin wanted to examine me (this was their second attempt to admit me to the Forensic Unit). To me this was a **conflict of interest** because we (Dr. Zin & I) never liked each other from their first attempted admittance. By the way, **my first admittance and offense**; through the court system, **I was dismissed** from going into the RPC Regional Forensic Unit to Dr. Zin's dismay (Dr. Zin is Satan in guise).

4-22-91:
Dr. Zin increased my medication without giving me proper basis or reason per my request.

By Mark C. Russell

Dr. Zin & Dr. Bloom M.D.'s (Forensic Unit Psychiatrists As of 3-27-91):

Dr. Zin (As of 3-27-91):

1   Per staff physician on 12-11-90, Notice of Status & Rights – Involuntary Status Form – this Form had incomplete names to send copies to.

2   Per Section 9.05 of the Mental Hygiene Law Part 3 (b) it says, "A certificate, as required by this article, must show that the person is mentally ill and shall be based on examination of the person alledged to be mentally ill made within ten days prior to the date of examination. "Dr. Zin has never done an examination on me nor has anybody else. I have been at the Forensic Unit 109 days (i.e. since 12-11-90) and I have never had treatment, care, or hospitalization. Dr. Zin has not done an evaluation, observed, or talked with me except to ask me how I'm doing; and I always reply, "fine, as always, have a good day." I've said very little even to other Staff. A doctor can't make any valid assumptions, conclusions, or judgements without talking to the source. Most of the information is from third party information, not mine.

3   Per Form, OMH 475 (MH) (1-89) page 2, "Application For Involuntary Admission or Certificate of a Director of Community Services or Designee" Section 9.37 Mental Hygiene Law, Dr. Zin states under part A, Application For Admission, "Patient has set fire on a shed for no apparent reason." Again, reasons are unknown for fire and Dr. Zin cannot make any psychotic assumptions; even to medicate me. Dr. Zin also states, "Has been acting suspicious and confused at jail, and, his suspicions don't have any insight towards his situation." Inside the Forensic Unit, at all times I minded my own business and was only suspicious given no one free phone call. I was only confused as to my placement at the Forensic Unit. Two things to note (1) per my notes, Dr. Zin says I am hearing voices and (2) I express my feelings to him for help. These are two outright lies!

4   Per Form, Notice of Application For Court Authorization To Retain A Patient, I received 1-14-91 by Dr. Zin; this Form had no "Date of Notice To Patient", no "names for Copies to send to", and no "reverse side " for "Certification of Service (Mental Illness)".

5   Per Form, 324 ADM (MH) (2-85); Record System Notification, this Form contained my incorrect Social Security Number.

6 Per Form, OMH 471(2-88) Page 4; I received this Form on 1-10-91 whereby it had my incorrect Social Security Number and no signature of Admitting Physician.

7 Per Form, 72-A ADM (2-77) N.Y.S. Department of Mental Hygiene – Inventory of Client's Personal Property; and Per Forensic Unit Handbook page 10, "Admission Procedures – personal items the person may have arrived with are sorted and a detailed list is made, a copy of which the patient is provided for their keeping." I came from jail with only the clothes on me. Diane, the Nurse, completed my Property Intake Form and put down that I had a Green Sweater upon arrival. To date, I never even owned a Green Sweater.

Note: There appears, from the immediate above, a major Internal Control Problem. This should definitely be addressed. To me this is just part of their System.

Dr. Bloom (As of 3-27-91):

1 Per Notice of "Status & Rights Form - Conversion To Involuntary Status", there included on this Form was a wrongly printed date (i.e. December 1, 1990) which should have been stated as December 13,1990; typical/indicative of such a system, wouldn't you say?

2 This same Form (Part A. above) had written on it (Sec. 9.13 (b), M.H. Law). This states that I'm Voluntary Admitted to the Forensic Unit; instead it should read Involuntary Admitted. This is another typical mistake.

3 Dr. Bloom converted me to The Forensic Unit on 12-13-90 whereby I would not talk to him (my legal right). Dr. Bloom per Affidavit in support of Application To Treat Over Objection dated 1-16-91 says, Dr. Bloom is familiar with me in that he reviewed my medical records and "by interviewing the patient". The doctor never "interviewed me". I've only been in contact with Dr. Bloom once or twice and only to say, I'm exercising my legal right not to talk to him. To me this is the Blind Leading The Blind; what a farce.

CHAPTER 7

Incompetencies And Improprieties
Rochester Regional Forensic Unit
Involuntary Treatment Court Hearing (3-28-91)
Another Great Satan System

DR. ZIN M. D. (FORENSIC UNIT PSYCHIATRIST) HALL OF JUSTICE ROCHESTER, NEW YORK

Dr. Zin (Psychiatrist) Versus Mr. Mark C. Russell (Defendant)
Dialogue Per Court Transcript In Reference To RPC Regional Forensic Unit:

Page No. 4:
"An order was entered which found that my client was not competent at the present time..." At the **"Competency Hearing"** my Public Defender Ms. Bell and three psychiatrists started to ask me questions concerning issues that were beyond the scope of their inquiry or exam. They started asking me things such as did I submit documents and read documents concerning the FBI in court and do I feel the FBI has anything to do with the crime and alleged crime committed. I said I was shown a letter to the FBI and said the signature was mine but I did not read the letter. As for the other questions I said that I was not in a court of law and felt they were going beyond their scope. Where was my so-called lawyer... asleep? Even use of the Mental Hygiene Legal Service (MHLS), my lawyer, was able to stop such questioning. **Why did Ms. Bell (My Public Defender) remain silent? I understand that a competency exam was to see if I (1) know the charges; (2) know the penalties; (3) be able to behave in court; (4) know peoples jobs in court; and (5) discuss strategies with my Attorney.** During the Competency Hearing there was not much if at all any conversation between my lawyer and me. I showed the Psychiatrists copies of the NYS Penal Law Section 150.10 (i.e. Arson 3rd Degree) and told them without looking at the paperwork the possible sentence term of which Ms. Bell said and told me on 2-24-90. **None of the other four criteria were presented to me.** I believe I passed their so-called brief test with flying colors. At one point, the one psychiatrist thought I was having trouble. I asked this psychiatrist to name anything, specifically, that I was having so called trouble with. He could not answer me but Dr. Took broke in and mentioned I did not go downtown. I said that they wanted me to go downtown on the spot with no preparation. This whole episode was, in my opinion, not professionally handled. This was just a part of a system designed to squelch me and my Government episode; a system within a system or systems. In my professional opinion they came to a wrong conclusion whether voluntary or involuntary!

Page No. 15:
"Doctor, based upon the examinations that you have conducted of Mr. Russell, and based upon your observations of him..." Never has Dr. Zin

examine me nor has he observed me. I only recall that Dr. Zin had twice came into the Dayroom and stayed approximately fifteen minutes; nothing more. Either way, Dr. Zin has never examined or observed me and he is making wrong judgement calls with no basis and only within the scope of third party information submitted to him.

Page No. 15:
"I believe that he suffers from Bipolar Effective Disorder keeping in mind that I would like to rule out Delusional Disorder". How can a person make any valid assumptions, observations, or conclusions when the patient has not even sat down to talk to a doctor? There was never dialogue between patient and doctor. Also, I've had other psychiatrists say I'm Delusional. **"When we do not have enough information, objectively, subjectively, to make the diagnosis according to that diagnosis manual..."** Even Dr. Zin admitted that he does not have enough information to make a proper diagnosis. It sounds like we have an over zealous Dr. Zin. He is digging for gold!

Page No. 17:
"...and later the parents went down there and Mr. Russell was clearly delusional". Dr. Zin contradicts his diagnosis via above (Page 15 he says he rules out Delusional Disorder and on pages 17 & 45 he says I'm Delusional). Stupidity and incompetent! I'd like to sue!

Page No. 45:
"...the basis of your decision that he suffers mental illness in this case Paranoid Delusional?" I think Dr. Zin is incompetent because at one point he rules out Delusional Disorder and later he says I've got a Paranoid Delusional Disorder. I really think that Dr. Zin thinks he is a legend in his own mind and is incompetent and nonsensical. I don't believe Dr. Zin has the capacity to make a reasoned judgement concerning myself! Again, I'd like to sue!

Page No. 18:
"He went and saw a psychiatrist who had some qualifications with the Navy in the war." I saw Dr. Seyless (my first psychiatrist ever) about five or less times. My parents and me did not like this psychiatrist; to me, he only served the interests of the Government (NAVY). Dr. Seyless restricted me from saying little if anything at all. How do you understand the problem if you don't communicate? The last time I was in contact with Dr. Seyless he asked me if I was still Delusional and if my thought patterns changed. I said no, and that I was not Delusional. After this, Dr.

Seyless then said, **"Ah Fuck, I guess I will have to write that down"**. This in itself is indicative; I was dealing with a MORON.

Page No. 21:
"I will be more than happy to sit down and discuss it with you. You convince me. That's your ticket to get out." Dr. Zin falsely put me into the Forensic Unit. Because of this, I think Dr. Zin was over zealous and he did not like me. The reason I did not talk to him was because I did not want to give him any more ammunition to twist both our interests. In other words he screwed up already enough on me!

Page No. 22:
"I have personally seen Mr. Russell talking to himself." Seldom do I talk to myself and if so, it's insignificant. Dr. Zin is looking for anything to discredit me. I, for example, have seen RPC staff talk to themselves; specifically, Ms. Day (Staff-FPA). This does not make her psychotic!!

Page No. 25:
"...does Mr. Russell have the capacity to make a reasoned judgement about whether or not to take this medication?" I do have this capacity. I also have a reasoned judgement to initiate this court proceeding and to provide evidence and facts to determine Dr. Zin's incompetence. I believe Dr. Zin is a liar and is perjuring. I am however, Paranoid that the Government is following me and is **illegally** harassing me as I can prove with past experiences with the FBI and NIS. I don't believe Dr. Zin has the capacity to make a reasoned judgement concerning myself.

Page No. 28:
Dr. Zin said he wanted me to **"go back to my job."** On the contrary, and in my **PROFESSIONAL** opinion I could never go back to my job. Dr. Zin is an **idiot** and an **asshole!!!!!!!!!!!!!**

Page No. 30:
"...they were doing some work in the back yard with some metal detectors and he was scared." There was nothing out of the ordinary on my part. How many times do you get someone with a metal detector in your backyard? I think this goes without saying and I believe the Government had a part in this episode.

Page No. 31:
"Usually, when it comes to visits, he usually has some problem with the visits and staff have to come in and set limits on him." This simply is not true. I've never had limits set on me! LIAR!

Page No. 32 & 41& 42:
"...last week, I come in and I see that he has a kind of bruise and abrasion on his face." "The bruise that you mentioned, do you have a guess, medical guess on how that injury occurred? Do you have any medical opinion as to how that bruise occurred on his face?" There was no bruise; it was only a nick from shaving. Dr. Zin exaggerates this story and is digging for gold. He thought my nick could be infected and that I need a tetanus shot. Dr. Zin thought that I might get ischemia (I think Dr. Zin is Paranoid and needs to seek help from another psychiatrist). Dr. Zin is definitely over zealous. My shaving nick healed as normal and expected **(it's only a nick)**. Again, Dr. Zin is over zealous and incompetent. I don't believe Dr. Zin has the capacity to make a reasoned judgement concerning myself.

Page No. 36:
"He impresses me like somebody who enjoys the security of being there and I think that was the case... He enjoys the security of being in the hospital... and the attention of the doctor going to talk to him, but at the same time, he enjoys telling them that, "I don't want to talk to you."" I don't enjoy these things. If I enjoy the security of being in the hospital then why do I go to court trying to get out of the hospital and why do I try to avoid the Staff at the Forensic Unit? In fact, I hate being there and hate the so-called security. Several times, in fact, I did tell Dr Zin this fact. Dr. Zin is a liar!

Page No. 38 & 39:
"...having Mr. Russell with a lot of facial expressions, a lot of anger, not following the rules again and again, coming up knowing that he should not intervene with the patients who are coming up again and doing that, yes he could get dangerous. Q. But he hasn't; is that right? A. Well, the possibility is almost zero." Dr. Zin contradicts himself by saying yes, he could get dangerous and right after this he says, well, the possibility is almost zero. I have not a lot of facial expressions, or anger; any for that matter. I think that Dr. Zin is nonsensical and incompetent. Dr. Zin is Satan in guise.

Page No. 40:
"Mr. Russell was not following the rules. He was supposed to be in the dayroom and he wanted to go out of the dayroom...He was supposed to be in the dayroom but he wanted to leave the dayroom at the time he was not supposed to... No, he was willing to leave the dayroom. He was directed to stay in the dayroom but he wanted to leave the dayroom?... Do you know what reason, why he wanted to stay in the dayroom?" Dr. Zin contradicts himself by saying I want to go out of the dayroom and on the same transcript page says, I wanted to stay in the dayroom. I feel very much that Dr. Zin is nonsensical and incompetent! Again, Satan in guise.

Page No. 44:
"...talked about sarcasm and suspicion and irritable and angry and doesn't follow rules..." Sarcasm, suspicion, and irritability are all not significant to even bat an eye. Dr. Zin is digging for gold! Again, I followed all rules.

Page No. 45:
"...coming across with some reasons rather than accusing the Government of putting wires on the doors, rather than accusing the Government of sending some waves through the radio of the car in order to cause spouses getting divorced, rather than Governments manipulating the EEG machine in order to create some waves in one's mind. These are pretty delusional. Q. But Possible?" As for the Government putting wires on the front door, my older brother verified to me that someone was tampering with my brand new lock on my door. The Government can easily transmit their own radio waves to anybody's radio, stereo, etc. for whatever their use may be (as was verified to me by co-workers Mathew and Tipper). And the Government's technology can easily manipulate an EEG machine to distort the resultant waves. OH, REMEMBER, THESE ITEMS ARE NOT DELUSIONAL BECAUSE DR. Zin HAD RULED OUT DELUSIONAL DISORDER (See reference Page No. 15 above).

Page No. 46:
"No, I don't think, anybody through an EEG machine, can manipulate anybody's mind... the world would not be safe if there was that kind of thing." How do you, Dr. Zin, know underlying things that happen in a TOP SECRET WORLD? "The world would not be safe if there was that kind of thing..." In fact, for your information Dr. Zin, our world is not safe! Just open your eyes, Dr. Zin, you are still living in the DARK AGES!

Page No. 54:
"...does his position of a holder of a Master's Degree, to what extent does that lend to that decision? None at all. I'm a physician. I treat a patient. He could have not told me he has a Master's Degree. I would still feel the same way I feel now. I don't believe any patient should stay in the hospital." I highly doubt this; Dr. Zin wanted me to go back to my old job without any input from me. I, in fact, and contrary to Dr. Zin, absolutely do not want to go back to my old job! I have no reservation whatsoever under any circumstances want to go back to my old job! Dr. Zin is an asshole and in my opinion is incompetent!

JUDGE COX & MR. CONN (MENTAL HYGIENE LEGAL SERVICE (MHLS) - ATTORNEY)

Involuntary Treatment Court Hearing
Hall of Justice Rochester, New York (3-28-91):

1   Judge Cox would not let me use my Bible on which to swear in for testimony.

2   The judge would not let me read my four and a half page speech to answer the question, **"Is there anything more I would like to say concerning why I feel I should not be medicated?"** I had to rely on Mr. Conn's narrowly tailored questions of which Mr. Conn had no idea what was in my four and one half page speech. I say this impropriety is Mr. Conn's (Attorney) fault for he told me prior to the Court hearing I would be able to answer the above question with no restrictions (the restriction being a speech). Based on this I was not given the **proper rights to** the proposed treatment and its **objections** to be **FULLY REVIEWED** by the Court. Everybody, in retrospect, knew of this to be an impropriety relative to lack of **DUE PROCESS** guaranteed in the 14th Amendment of our Constitution; this atrocity and lack of jurisprudence includes both the Judge (Honorable Cox) and my attorney (Mr. Conn).

3   I told Judge Cox that I have evidence (Forms) to prove Dr. Zin incompetent as well as Dr. Bloom (e.g. incomplete forms with some forms with wrong information). The Judge would not let me admit any documents to prove their incompetence; where was my attorney during this? I said to the Judge I could prove the incompetence of the doctors. **Judge Cox said, "No. I'm taking your word for it at this point."** The Judge never brought the subject up again (e.g. during the court hearing) and he ultimately ruled against me. **If he took my word for it, he would not have ruled against me!!** I feel that the Judge was practicing the profession fraudulently, through gross incompetence and or negligence. The Judge knew my attorney was not prepared to ask more questions relative to my speech and my Defense. Satan might as well been the judge.

Note: I did not have a chance in Hell against the immediate above; what do you think?

CHAPTER 8

Incompetencies And Improprieties
Rochester Regional Forensic Unit Staff
(1990-1993)
Dr. Sing, Mr. Cent, and Miscellaneous Staff
Another Great Satan System

DR. SING, M. D. (1991 – 1993 PSYCHIATRIST –FROM MY OWN RECORD OF PAGE NUMBERED NOTES):

Page No. 1 (10-01-91):

Dr. Sing said I would be out of the RPC Regional Forensic Unit in a matter of days; then one and one half weeks later he said I would get out of the Forensic Unit 4-6 weeks, and later to get out indefinitely. To me, he was toying with me. He said I need to understand more from where other people are coming from to be competent. Merely, this is more lies concerning my competency.

Page No. 5 (10-23-91):

Via meeting, Dr. Sing's diagnosis was Schizophrenic Bipolar Disorder. Later, Dr. Sing said it's not Schizophrenic Bipolar Disorder.

Page No. 7 (10-30-91):

Dr. Sing rarely had first hand observation of me, as was also the case with Dr. Zin. This was his first time of direct observation. He for the second time did the same the next day (on 10-31-91 Dr. Sing briefly came into the Dayroom). On 11-08-91 Dr. Sing again briefly came into the Dayroom.

Page No. 18 (12-10-91):

Met with Dr. Sing, Dr. Cione, and two students (Jennifer & Michele). They asked some questions. Dr. Sing said I need more medicine and then mental illness will subside. I'm still trying to figure out specifically what mental illness. I also gave Dr. Sing a copy of "TIME MAGAZINE"dated 11-11-91 to read: entitled, "Somebody's Watching How Business, Government, and even the folks next door are tracking your secrets." This magazine only proves Dr. Sing's unworldly neglect, wantonness, and stupidity!

Page No. 20 (12-18-91):

I took Prolixin and suffered muscle tightness. Dr. Sing never asked me of any side effects. I had to tell him. He should have been on top of this situation for possible Cogentin medication.

Page No. 23 (12-31-91):

Dr. Sing did not agree with Dr. Zin's diagnosis of Bipolar Disorder per conversation.

Page No. 24 (1-08-92):
Dr. Sing increased my meds while other staff said I'm doing fine. There seems to be a contradiction here!

Page No. 26 (1-15-92):
I was told to convince Ms. Bell (Public Defender) and Dr. Sing that I'm doing well enough to be competent to stand trial; there were no specifics to this. They are playing with my mind!!

Page No. 30 (2-07-92):
Ms. Bell (Public Defender) and Dr. Sing thought I was competent and would like me to get out of the Forensic Unit as soon as possible. Ms. Bell said either next Monday or next Tuesday. It never happened.

Page No. 31 (12-13-92):
Again, Dr. Sing said I was doing very good and he says he has my case on his mind indicating, again, he is closer to writing his report for me to get out of the Forensic Unit.

Page No. 32 (12-20-92):
Dr. Sing thought Ms. Bell (Public Defender) said she was leaning towards me pleading Mental Defect or Disease at the time of crime. I only said I would consider this plea, not, that I flatly would do this. I said I would consider this plea among other alternatives but at the bottom of alternatives. Because I said this, Dr. Sing checked and told me there could be one more year, in the Forensic Unit, if I did not take the Mental Defect or Disease plea. I believe Dr. Sing to be manipulative!!

Page No. 37 & 38 (3-26-92 & 4-03-92):
Dr. Sing said my time applies towards Forensic Unit as time served at jail. Ms. Marvin (Staff) disagreed. Come to find out, Dr. Sing was wrong. Ms. Bell (Public Defender) changed her mind and said that the time spent at the Forensic Unit does not go towards jail time served. Dr. Sing thought the same. They are feeding me with false information and I consider them both to be incompetent and lack the capacity to make reasoned judgements concerning my case.

Page No. 39 (4-05-92):
I reminded Ms. Bell and Dr. Sing in reference to above note (pages 37 & 38) that they were incompetent.

Page No. 42 (4-24-92):

In June I was scheduled to go to court and Dr. Sing said he is going to say that I'm still mentally ill based on one assumption and that is by the Government tapping my phones, and their surveillance of me. The FBI and the NIS did this surveillance of me once before why not now (I even showed Dr. Sing a written letter as evidence to prove their investigation – See APPENDIX of FBI/NIS letter)? Even per evidence, Dr. Sing is still naïve and incompetent. This, in effect, is another system; Satan's System! These people are a bunch of snakes.

Page No. 43 (5-01-92):

Dr. Sing told me I could get a second opinion on my competency to stand trial. Per Mental Hygiene Legal Services (MHLS) this was not a means. I believe Dr. Sing to be incompetent by putting false information into my head. Again, Dr. Sing is manipulative, naïve, and a snake!!

Mr. Cent – Chief of Service RPC Forensic Unit;
Notes-Page Nos. 152-3 (4-15-91):

Mr. Cent (Chief of Service RPC Forensic Unit) approached me to find out more information about my nine-page letter of Abuses/Mistreatments. Tony said the Director delegated his responsibility to Tony to investigate the situation concerning the Abuses/Mistreatments. But the Law states (per Mental Hygiene Law Section 7.21 (b)) that "such Director shall have the responsibility of seeing that there is humane treatment of the patients...and shall investigate every case of alleged patient abuse." As is opposed to Mental Hygiene Law per Section 9.33 which states, " The Director shall cause written notice...." Per Mental Hygiene Law the Director should have done the investigation. Since one of my reported Abuses/Mistreatments involved Mr. Cent, there is a "Conflict of Interest" and the concept of "Independence" falls face down or is shot. WHY? Because Mr. Cent was an integral part of one of the reported Abuses/Mistreatments. My Attorney, Mr. O'Donnell (Mental Hygiene Legal Service-MHLS) agreed with me that there was a conflict of interest and lack of independence but, for some reason, Mr. O'Donnell's Superior did not agree with Mr. O'Donnell and myself (this is Satan's System at its best!). I don't think Dr. Mark Van Zolden (Director), Mr. Cent, or Mr. O'Donnell's Superior is competent to make reasoned decisions concerning my behalf or others! AGAIN, A GOOD CONSPIRACY IS ONE THAT CAN'T BE PROVEN!!

OTHER MISCELLANEOUS STAFF (FORENSIC UNIT):

A. Deputy Dunn – UPON ADMISSION (12-11-90):

Per RPC Regional Forensic Unit myself, a nurse (Cat), Deputy Dunn, and another Deputy were present. The two Deputies stood around me and were yelling/screaming at me repeatedly. They said I was not cooperating by not answering their medical background questions. They, in essence were telling me I was doing a wrong by saying that I'm not cooperating when, in fact, I was doing a right by exercising a legal right not to answer so called medical background questions. I again, several times throughout their so-called interrogation told them I'm exercising my right not to answer their medical background questions. Per RPC Regional Forensic Unit Handbook page eleven it says, "All admissions are done as professionally as possible and at a relatively relaxing pace to assist the person in reducing their fears and anxieties and to begin the first step toward a trusting, therapeutic relationship with staff." This definitely was not the case (Satan was acting overtime here!).

A.1. Mr. Dunn (1-11-91):

Mr. Dunn said, under Criminal Procedure Laws 730 and 330.20 your property is automatically transferred to RPC Forensic Unit but under 508 Correction Law your property stays at the jail. According to the Forensic Unit Patient Handbook page 10 and 11 it doesn't state any distinction for transfer of property relative to Correction Law and Criminal Procedure Law. But does plainly state property will be transferred and patient will receive a receipt upon arrival/processing. Mr. Cent (Chief of Service – Forensic Unit) should rewrite the Handbook to account for this distinction. Of course, a Mr. Cent has no intellect to do such a task.

A.2. Mr. Dunn (4-04-91):

Mr. Dunn approached me at 7:30 PM and said downstairs they had my money totaling $149.00 to put into the commissary and I said this was the wrong dollar amount. I said it should be $143.95 and showed Mr. Dunn my deposit slip of Monroe County's Sheriff's Account (No. MC-041996) showing this amount dated 12-08-90. Mr. Dunn said the most I can have in my Commissary Account was $100.00. Mr. Dunn said he would make note and relay my Account as $143.95. Mr. Dunn asked me if I want the amount over $100.00 be given to my parents or other. I said no. Mr. Dunn said he would relay this to the people downstairs and get back to me. The Forensic Unit Handbook, per pages 27-29 only mentions a "patient's account" with no cash or money limit (i.e. $100.00). I've been at the Forensic Unit for 116 days now; why the transfer now?

B. Ms. Bane – Aide (12-18-90):

I was put in solitary quiet room without cause or basis by Ms. Bane. I never have gotten a "Rights of Inpatients in Psychiatric Center NYS Office of Mental Health Handbook". I ONLY asked Ms. Bane for a copy, as I should have upon ADMISSION. She only claims that I was harassing her which was definitely not true! Per Dr. Rank, she said I should have gotten a Handbook (which was available) and is contrary to what Ms. Bane said that there was not an available Handbook. Being put into Solitary confinement, to me, was untherapeutic and not called for; HOW BARBARIC!

B.1. Ms. Bane (1-03-91):

Ms. Bane, as you may know, had it in for me. She came over to my lunch table where myself and Harold (patient) were sitting. Ms. Bane said, "Harold, put your false teeth back into your mouth. Mark (myself) thinks this to be distasteful also." I hadn't said a thing until then and then I said, " I don't think it to be distasteful". Harold always washes his dentures in his milk carton after he eats. Ms. Bane yelled at me for saying what I had said and threatened to give me a violation. Subsequently, I started conversation with Harold about a world event. Ms. Bane again being provacative said world events are not appropriate conversations and threatened me again with another possible violation. I then proceeded to ask her if I should say anything to Harold so that I may not interfere with her or Harold. Ms. Bane could not give me a straight answer. So I left it at that.

B.2. Ms. Bane (1-09-91):

Staff are constantly telling patients not to talk loud across the room. Because of this, I told Ms. Bane not to talk loud across the room. I was being polite at the same time by saying to Ms. Bane to smile and that it was a blessed day. Ms. Bane being arrogant as can be expected responded to me by saying 'I'm hallucinating because of this'. To me, Ms. Bane is an idiot.

B.3. Ms. Bane (1-18-91):

According to Hospital Policy / Law, smoking in the cafeteria for smokers is "designated" from 12:30 to 1:30 PM. Everyone (smokers and nonsmokers), after naptime (i.e.1: 30 PM) congregate in the cafeteria before returning to the Dayroom. Ms. Bane was smoking (approximately at 1:38

PM) in front of nonsmokers; a clear violation of Policy/Law. As usual, Ms. Bane was trying to give me a hard time.

C. Ms. Bider — Aide (12-15-90):

Ms. Bider asked me why I did not help set up the Christmas tree. I said because two psychiatrists (namely Dr. Zin) stuck me here with improper basis (falsely) and against my will. I had previously taken these doctors to Court in reference to, not having Involuntary Care, at the Forensic Unit and I won my case. Ms. Bider got frustrated at me and was belittling me by telling others that I was incapable of answering simple questions. I wasn't incapable, but I simply did not want to cater to her manipulations; simply I was put here falsely.

C.1. Ms. Bider (12-25-90):

I've been in the Forensic Unit for 42 days and Ms. Bider now made it mandatory to work in order to get snacks at night. This represents another Staff member dictating policy at will.

C.2. Ms. Bider (1-01-91):

Ms. Bider approached me at 10:00 PM and asked if anyone needed newly clean clothes (the first time someone had asked). I said I needed clothes but had asked two other Aides long ago (i.e. Ms. Brent and Ms. Haw) and they said they would take care of it. Ms. Bider then said she was going to write down I refused clothes. I said no and won't refuse them if they were given to me. My point being, I've been waiting two weeks for these asked clothes and told Ms. Bider I do not refuse her getting me clothes. I still needed clothes. Why the long wait?

C.3. Ms. Bider ((1-16-91):

Ms. Sewart (Aide) and Ms. Bider (Aide) were asked at the same time if I could get a pen. They both said in a minute. I went into the Recreation Room and about five minutes later Mr. Mass (Aide) came into the room and opened the locker with pens in it. I asked him if he could give me a pen. He said yes. Ms. Bider yelled at me for asking Mr. Mass even after Mr. Mass had counted all ten pens for security and looked to Ms. Sewart and Ms. Bider and said he had counted ten pens. Ms. Bider said I'm manipulative by making Mr. Mass intercede instead of waiting for her or Ms. Sewart. Mr. Mass always issues pens and he was available so I asked him. Then again, Ms. Bider said to wait for her and not Mr. Mass. Then Mr. Mass comes back fifteen minutes later and says he will give me a pen. Obviously, there is no communication here. Then Ms. Sewart comes into the room and says let's get a pen. I said to Ms. Sewart what is the difference if I asked Mr. Mass first of all instead of Ms. Sewart and Mr. Mass to get me the pen and did a security check? Ms. Sewart then said, "none". Can you see my predicament?

C.4. Ms. Bider (1-26-91):

I saw Ms. Bider sitting on the endtable while supervising the patients. On page 16 of the RPC Forensic Unit Patient Level Handbook "Expectations" it says, "ward expectations are things that we expect every patient to do. These expectations involve respect for yourself, for others, and for your environment and, in general, behaving in an adult manner." "(1) You will not put your feet on the furniture because we are trying to maintain a clean environment for everyone." Time and time again people have been told not to sit on tables as well. What makes Ms. Bider special and what kind of example is she setting?

C.5. Ms. Bider (2-12-91):

Ms. Bider DENIED my visit. Ms. Harter (Aide) was going to take me downstairs to my visit when I asked if she could call down and see who the visitor was so I can refuse or accept the visit. Ms. Harter said no. I started to discuss it with her and the Deputy and I said I've been here over two months and every time I've had a visit the Aides would call downstairs to see who it was. I asked why the sudden change. Then Ms. Bider rudely called me back into the dayroom (from the hallway) and broke into my conversation with Ms. Harter and the Deputy. I obeyed Ms.Bider and asked if she could call downstairs to see who was visiting me. Ms. Bider said no and denied me the right to this visit. HOW BARBARIC!

C.6. Ms. Bider (4-14-91):

In my previous notes in a community meeting dated 1-07-91 it says, "the final decision/policy by Ms. Sittco and Ms. Marvin (Aides), was 30 minutes to eat from the last person to get their tray and food after going through the lunch line." I was about the last person in the lunch line and 15 minutes expired (from the last person in lunch/dinner line (i.e. myself). I told Ms. Bider the Policy, as described, from the community meeting on 1-07-91 (i.e. 30 minutes rule). Ms. Bider said it is her policy at will to hurry people up disregarding a community meeting conclusion. I told Ms. Bider I had an extra 15 minutes to eat and not have to devour the food. She then mandatorily told me to take my tray up. I then requested her to see my notes as documented, but, Ms. Bider denied my request. On page 2 of the "Rights of Inpatients it says,"A limitation of any of your rights must be based on clinical justifications that have been explained to you and documented in your clinical record, with specific time the limitation will remain in effect."

Later, during Clothes for Shower I was walking back to the cafeteria from the Dorm and had walked between Ms. Bider and a patient and Ms. Bider did not want me to get close to her (for whatever reason). Ms. Bider said I was being sarcastic when trying to prove the above that I was right (but so what?). I asked Ms. Bider what sarcasm?; she wouldn't answer me because she did not know. Ms. Bider then put me into the Dayroom followed by putting me in the Quiet Room in the dark (no lights) even after I had asked to put the lights on. I was put into the Quiet Room for approximately one hour. This was barbaric and inappropriate, and illegal treatment.

C.7. Ms. Bider (1-01-92):

My parents and sister came to visit me at the Forensic Unit. Ms. Bider was trying to hear my conversation with my family. I told my family that nonsmokers had to be in company with smokers (while smoking) to bring in the New Year. Because I said this Ms. Bider was going to record what I said. Ms. Bider had to have super ears and diligence to invade my privacy (while talking to my parents). Bottom line: Ms. Bider had no right to invade my privacy. On the way back to the Dayroom Ms. Bider was trying to tell me what I can or cannot say to my parents. This is plainly not right per Patient Rights Handbook; we are allowed privacy when visited. Ms. Bider blatantly overstepped her bounds.

D. Mr. Sandal – Aide (12-27-90):

Mr. Sandal has been swearing while talking to other staff. Mr. Sandal swears around staff and patients (e.g. motherfucker, asshole, etc.). I've heard Mr. Sandal swear during the sleeping /night shift as well. I'm appalled at his behavior! Satan's system at work!

E. Ms. Lark - Aide (12-27-90):

The Aides, Ms. Lark and Mr. Sandal, were not familiar with Mental Hygiene Laws and how to attain such Laws. I believe the Mental Hygiene Laws should be readily accessible and that Staff should know some basics concerning these matters.

E.1. Ms. Lark (12-29-90):

There were only two patients in the Dayroom plus Ms. Lark. I went to the TV set to find a station. I asked the other patient if I could change the channel and the patient said yes. Ms. Lark said no that I could not change the station; I only could change on the hour. Ms. Lark was dictating policy at will. Other Staff's policy was to take the patient's vote.

E.2. Ms. Lark (1-10-91):
Aides Ms. Lark and Ms. Brent were asked to call downstairs later to find out the time of escort for my Court hearing at night (6:00 PM scheduled). Later, Ms. Lark and Ms. Brent said they would not call down stairs because it was not in their job descriptions. In the past other Staff would call down stairs with no problem and find out ahead of time the time of my escort. Ultimately, Barbara (the nurse) said she would be glad to call down and she did so. There seems to be different and confusing policies.

E.3. Ms. Lark (1-11-91):
Per Rights of Inpatients ... in Psychiatric Centers of the NYS Office of Mental Health page 14 it says, "All patients have a right to object any form of care and treatment and to appeal decisions with which they disagree." Ms. Lark asked if I wanted to play a game with her. The point is she is repeatedly harassing me by asking me over and over to play. She then proceeded to argue with me and every time I would say, "no". She even went to the point where she said she would cry if I did not play. My point is that Ms. Lark should have left me alone from her relentless pursuit.

E.4. Ms. Lark (2-22-91):
To show how stupid the mentality and reliability Staff were, Ms. Lark, led us (i.e. nonsmokers) from the cafeteria after lunch to the Dayroom. Before we got to the Dayroom, Ms. Lark, remembered that we were supposed to go to the Dorm to take our daily naps; as always (i.e. 12:30 – 1:30). Ms. Lark is senile. How can an institution run properly with such decadence?

E.5. Ms. Lark (2-27-91):
Ms. Lark said I did not hand in my pen per her instructions and that I was very insulting when discussing the matter with her. I did ask Ms. Lark if she wanted my pen just to be safe. Ms. Lark did not answer me. I kept the pen a little longer (maybe five minutes) and handed it in at approximately 2:50 PM. It's Ms. Lark standard usually to collect non-smokers pens at 3:00PM and at 2:45PM she usually collects pens from the smokers. She only confused me because she was going against her prior standards of collecting pens. To me, just harassment! Only a Satanic system!

E.6. Ms. Lark (3-09-91):

Ms. Lark gave me a Minor Violation for the following: I had asked Ms. Lark if I was on the laundry list for that day. Ms. Lark said she had no record of my dirty laundry (in the Soiled Linen Room) where everyone keeps their dirty laundry on either numbered hooks or your name tag (numbers and names are on the white sticker above your laundry hook). I said I saw my dirty laundry on the number four hook last evening (marked not by number 4 but by my name, Mark C. Russell) at shower time. I said I never take my dirty laundry out of that room (I've been here 90 days to date). Ms. Day (Aide) and I went down to see if my dirty laundry was there. My dirty laundry was missing and my name tag/ sticker was switched to hook number 2 from number 4 hook. Empty laundry bags were on both hooks. My clothes were missing. I don't have a key to this locked room. Only Staff have keys. Staff always supervise and escort us to and from this room. The bottom line is I had nothing to do with my missing laundry and I certainly did not have tag stickers in order to switch hooks. I also documented that my hooknumber was number 4 and my locker number was number 4 switched to number 2. But now Staff switches my hook number on 3-08-91 (after showers) or on 3-09-91 (before 3:00PM). Ms. Lark, after trying to explain this to her said that Staff had nothing to do with this (i.e. missing dirty laundry and tag switch). I tried to debate the issue and Ms. Lark was stubborn and did not change her stance. We only discussed the matter for only a few minutes. Ms. Lark told me to be quiet (i.e. to stop talking or discussing) and said I ought to take medicine. I said she was out of line. Then Ms. Lark wrongfully punished me by putting me out in the hallway (I went without speaking a word). Five minutes later I was let back into the Dayroom. Bottom Line: my laundry (possessions) were missing and never returned to me and I believe it was Staff's fault. Indicative, Staff did nothing.

E.7. Ms. Lark (4-14-91):

Ms. Lark stated to me that all levels can go to the Music/Library Room every night (i.e. 7:00 – 8:00PM) to get use of the phone book. In the past, the phonebooks were in either the Dayroom or Recreation Room; not in the Music/Library Room. Per page 21 of the Forensic Handbook, it states, "Three times a week the Library is open to all levels from 7:00 – 8:00 PM." Per page 23 of the same Handbook states, "The Library/ Music Room is open during the day and evening hours... In order to use the Music Room, one must be on Level 3". The debate was that Ms. Lark said the Music/ Library Room is open every night for all Levels from 7:00 – 8:00 PM. I told Ms. Lark that her statement was false. I even asked her to see the Patient Forensic Handbook to prove her wrong. Ms. Lark said she didn't want to see the Handbook. How arrogant, negligent, and manipulative.

E.8. Ms. Lark (1-12-92):
Once again, Ms. Lark was harassing me. During the operation of the drying clothing machine Ms. Lark told me to dry my clothes for 50 minutes. I told Ms. Lark that I've used the dryer for over a year now and 40 minutes has been fine for drying clothes... anything to harass me.

F. Ms. Day — Aide (12-28-90):
I feel that we should not be required to listen to music during breakfast, lunch, and dinner. Several times I had to hear hard rock songs. Dancing, per Ms. Day and Staff, has also been encouraged in the LunchRoom. What would happen if all patients danced in the LunchRoom during eating times? This seems to be a security risk; per Forensic Unit Handbook page 19 all patients are here on an Involuntary basis (i.e. mental illness and a danger to themselves or others). Per Forensic Unit Handbook page 9 states, "The security rules of the RRFU might at times seem strict and burdensome. However if one substitutes the word "safety" for the word "security" the rules may be easier to understand. The safety of all patients, staff members, and visitors is a primary concern to the Unit Administrators"; I believe dancing should be abolished.

F.1. Ms. Day (1-04-91):
Ms. Day and Mr. Sandal were arguing rather loud during the early morning sleeping hours. They were arguing over their own personal matters concerning a personal conflict between the two of them. First of all, I'd rather not here it and second, I'd like to sleep! Another words, get your act together!

F.2. Ms. Day (1-04-91):
Ms. Day was talking to Staff in the Dayroom while I was sitting in front of her and she said that John (patient) and myself had left the Dayroom and were not in the Dayroom. I pointed out to Ms. Day that it was only John that was out of the Dayroom. I believe she was trying to be provocative and instigating some sort of response from me.

G. Ms. Haw — Aide (1-01-91):
I was in the Recreation Room writing some notes and Ms. Haw came into the Room and thought I was on level 3. I definitely was not on level 3; yet. To date, after three weeks of being there, nobody has told me what level I'm on or if there has been a change in level status and why or

why not. Not only Ms. Haw but other Staff has had to ask patients what level there on. Levels system is a very important and intricate part of Internal Control designating privileges and system type activity. This lack of readily available knowledge of patient system levels is a blatant lack of Internal Control. Also, my notes dated 1-03-91 indicates this lack of Internal Control (i.e. lack of patient levels knowledge) involves Ms. Olsen (RN) and Mr. Mass (Aide) also.

G.1. Ms. Haw (2-01-91):
I believe Ms. Haw to be provacative. She was asking me when I go to the Bathroom (even in front of patients) though her records show that I do not go to the Bathroom from the "Dayroom". I had asked her to please not to ask me personal questions because I'm sure she wouldn't like it if I asked her when she goes to the Bathroom. By the way, her records were not accurate, correct, or reliable.

G.2 Ms. Haw (2-23-91):
Ms. Haw made a Harold (a patient) listen to TV. I believe it's against a patient's rights to make them watch or listen to the TV especially shows like M – TV, Teen Witch (a movie), The Exorcist, etc.. In my opinion, this type of thing is not therapeutic! Prove me wrong!

G.3. Ms. Haw (4-26-91):
I believe Ms. Haw to be provocative again. At cafeteria time (lunch) Ms. Haw never called me for a shower or ADL'S (i.e. washing). I had asked to take a shower but they ignored me. Again their records were not accurate, correct, or reliable.

G.4. Ms. Haw (5-06-91):
At approximately 7:30 AM was another provocative situation. I've been at the Forensic Unit for 147 days and Ms. Haw is now in conflict of normal policy of a warmer blanket on top of a heavier blanket. She wanted vice – versa. Again, provocative; how petty.

G.5. Ms. Haw (11-05-91):
Ms. Haw tells patients constantly that nobody is allowed to sit on certain furniture (only allowed to sit in chairs). This morning I saw both Ms. Day (Aide) and Ms. Haw (Aide) sitting on the desk tops at the first tier of the Men's Dorm. Staff are hypocrites because they don't practice what they preach and are setting bad examples.

H. Marrie – Aide (2-08-91):

After my visit with my mom, dad, and sister, Marrie thought I was being rude by asking her, "Who was going to escort me upstairs? I was not rude; I just asked who was going to take me upstairs from the visiting room. A little later a guard escorted me upstairs. There was no problem or scene except Marrie's psychotic perception of what was rude or not.

I. Mr. Wittson – Recreation Therapist (2-26-91):

Mr. Wittson asked me if I wanted to go to the Gym. I said no as always. The point is that to participate in an activity of the Gym you had to be on level 4. I'm at this time, on level 2. This is a huge Internal Control Weakness and a negligence problem on the part of Mr. Wittson and Staff. Again, the level system is a basic part to the system at the Forensic Unit and should dogmatically be followed.

I.1. Mr. Wittson (4-01-91):

Mr. Wittson wanted to know if I wanted to join the woodburning activity. I said no. Why would Mr. Wittson ask an alleged arsonist, one that is mentally ill and dangerous, join a woodburning class? Is Mr. Wittson (thinking in terms of Doctor Zin), competent to make reasoned decisions concerning this matter and, accordingly, Dr. Zin should instruct Mr. Wittson to take medication for his psychosis in this matter?

J. Ms. Olsen – RN (2-19-91):

Ms. Olsen the other day scolded a patient for not signing out the time (erasing the time) on the blackboard. Ms. Olsen did not even look to see the time was erased. She just scolded the patient. Even upon looking at the blackboard and seeing that it was in fact erased she did not even say she was sorry!

J.1. Ms. Olsen (5-14-91):

I received a Minor Violation for the following: I was last in the breakfast line and when I got my food tray I went to look for a seat in the cafeteria. I found an empty chair. I sat down to eat at this empty chair. About five minutes later a patient, Sterling, approached me and said that I took his seat. Sterling said he was seated there three minutes ago. We went back and forth on this issue. There was a discrepancy as to policy and I got the short end of the stick. A Minor Violation was not in order here. I only thought it was Staff's policy in which nobody else has the right to a seat once physically occupied.

K. Dr. Mark Vanzolden — Director RPC (4-06-91):

Per Mental Hygiene Law Section 9.07 it explicitly states, "the Director shall inform the patient in writing of his status, including the section of this chapter under which he is hospitalized, and of his rights under the article, including the availability of the Mental Hygiene Legal Service (MHLS)". I never received OMH Form 461 Status Section 9.37 of MHL and written status of Section 508 Correction Law, 730 Correction Law, and 9.27 Section of Mental Hygiene Law. Is Dr. Mark Vanzolden incompetent? As such, "The Director shall cause written notice...", per admission or conversion status.

L. Ms. Eve —Nurse (2-26-91):

At 4:00 PM Ms. Eve asked me if I had a pen out. I said no and she said OK. I asked her why she asked me if I had a pen. She again asked if I had a pen. I said no. We went in circles asking our questions. Pointedly, if I have a pen out in my name it would be on the signout sheet in front of Ms. Eve. She made no comment at this point. A few minutes later Ms. Eve approached me and said that she asked me because there was an extra pen. I said I didn't see the logic in her asking me because if she had an extra pen in the inventory there would not be this pen out. Ms. Eve said nothing to this and left. Also, inventory of pens is not done at 4:00 PM, it is usually done at 3:30PM or before dinner at 4:00 PM. As stated before, if I had a pen out it would have been on the signout sheet in front of her?

L.1. Ms. Eve (3-06-91):

At 6:45 PM just before my visit with my family, Ms. Eve took my folder and its contents and misplaced them. They were not found after misplacement. I feel staff are negligent (no policies). In my mind it was intentional!

M. Ms. Sittco — Social Worker (4-01-91):

Upon Ms. Marvin (Social Worker) coming into the dayroom, I decided to move and stay away from Ms. Marvin because I don't need her so called treatment and care of which is my legal right to refuse. Ms. Sittco said I did not have to move and that Ms. Marvin was not going to look at my notes. My point is is that I just didn't want any contact with her which is my right. Ms. Sittco is being arrogant and manipulative.

N. Ms. Sewart — Aide (12-12-90):

I was sitting at the diner table during lunch and I asked a Mike (patient) to please not sing at the dinner table. He said he has made this table and I had no right to ask him such a question. He then got up and came over to me and said he was going to kick my ass. I said go ahead and kick my ass. He then sat down and started singing again. I asked him to stop his singing. He said no. I said I think he was brought up in a barn. I then took my tray up to the kitchen and then Ms. Sewart (Aide) interceded and escorted me to the Quiet Room. Ms. Sewart did so with no reason or charge or discussion. Point being, "my Dad would have asked the same question as I did; was Mr. Brooks brought up in a barn?" Ms. Sewart is barbaric. I believe Mike to be in the wrong, not me.

N.1. Ms. Sewart (5-29-91):

I was making a legal phone call to my Attorney Mr. Cryant (Hyatt Legal Services) and wanted to leave him a message to Mr. Cryant's Receptionist. Ms. Sewart broke into my conversation with the Receptionist; she then took the phone away from me and left a message. Ms. Sewart plainly violated policy and rights.

O. Mr. Mass – Aide (12-22-90):

Harold is a mental illness patient and should not have verbal abuse including that of Mr. Mass instigating the verbal abuse. Mr. Mass would have patient (e.g. Peg), to tell Harold that Peg is his daughter. Mr. Harold becomes furious and yells out that Peg is not his daughter. All staff "laugh" at Harold because they think it's funny! The staff further abuses Harold by saying he is a grandfather and again being furious at this accusation. I was taught to laugh with a person to be therapeutic as opposed to laughing at a person. Refer To Mental Hygiene Law Chapter Section 201-second paragraph for therapeutic roles of all disciplines.

O.1. Mr. Mass (12-31-90):

In order to watch TV (that brought in the New Year) non-smokers had to watch TV with the smokers while they smoked; discrimination! Also, Mr. Mass was in the Dorm Room at 10:30 PM (during sleeping hours) and called Jim (patient) to discuss problems relating to Jim. I think that Mr. Mass could have handled this scenario diplomatically by waiting and in private discuss personal matters with Jim.

O.2. Mr. Mass (1-04-91):

Concerning pen policy; I was going to sign out a pen and Mr. Mass printed my name and pertinent information for pen signout. I have been told before that I'm required to put my signature. Without my signature there is a weakness of Internal Control. There is also a lack of communication and procedures as well as communication among Staff.

O.3. Mr. Mass (1-11-91):

Twice Mr. Mass broke into my conversation with my parents during visiting hours in the Visitation Room. Per Patient Rights Handbook: While you are at this hospital, you have Rights which may only be limited for clinical reasons which include; Receiving Visitors at reasonable times, having privacy when visited, and communicating freely with persons with in or outside the Hospital. In other words, stay out of my private conversations during visits with my parents.

O.4. Mr. Mass (3-09-91):

There was a discrepancy as to who was to get for me State Funded Clothes. Ms. Bider (FPA II) told Mr. Mass that she was in charge not Mr. Mass. Mr. Mass said he did not know she was the one that was in charge and that Ms. Day (FPA) told him to get my State Funded Clothes. I said there was Staff miscommunication and that Mr. Mass could have gotten me in trouble. This is typical miscommunication.

O.5. Mr. Mass (3-16-91):

The new floor installers at the Forensic Unit put my dresser in a different spot in the Dorm Room (when they finished). Mr. Mass told Ed (patient) and myself to move the dressers back ourselves because it was not Mr. Mass's job. I believe moving the furniture is someother person's job; like maintenance or the people who installed the new floor. I do not have Workman's Compensation.

P. Ms. Sewart & Ms. Brent — Aides (2-20-91):

Marcelle Jackson (a patient), I believe, from listening to arguments sometimes has to go to the bathroom in repeated frequency during a short period of time to relieve herself. On 2-20-91 she had to go "number one" really bad but staff (e.g. Ms. Sewart and Ms. Brent) would not let her go. Staff told her no because she already went several times in the last hour, but even so, this does not solve Marcelle's problem by not letting her go. Because of staff's unloving, unprofessional, and ignorant attitude, Marcelle went "number one" on the dayroom floor to relieve herself. First of all, not letting her go doesn't solve the problem (she still has to go... bad), secondly, a health problem is created when "number one" is all over the dayroom floor and rug, and third, several of the patients don't care to watch Marcelle go "number one" in front of everybody (staff are BARBARIC)!

Q. Ms. Marvin – Social Worker (12-19-90):

Ms. Marvin started to walk me to the phone to call an Attorney of my choice for my case; I inquired to Ms. Marvin as to not having contact with her while making my legal phone call. After this inquiry, Ms. Marvin got upset and then said she did not want to talk to me. Ms. Marvin then left me without myself making a legal phone call. How petty and rude.

Q.1. Ms. Marvin (1-14-91):

I've brought the subject of Staff addressing and distinguishing a Mr. Mark Russell (myself) with that of a Mr. Robert Russell (another patient) on both 12-30-90 and 1-11-91 and several unnoted discussions. I've been in the Forensic Unit over 60 days and have asked Staff repeatedly to distinguish between us "Russells". Robert Russell is being called upon repeatedly by Staff and when Staff calls "Mr. Russell" (most times it's Robert) I have to look up everytime and say, "What". This becomes annoying to me because I rarely am being called upon; it's Mr. Robert Russell not me. I asked Ms. Marvin if it was reasonable to request to distinguish between us "Russells" when called upon. Ms. Marvin said, "This is a trick question". Ms. Marvin, after several prior requests, finally said it was a reasonable request and would look into it. A final note; Staff put Robert's and mine beds next to each other to confuse matters even more.

R. Dr. Bloom – Forensic Unit Psychiatrist – (1-17-91):

At a Community Meeting at 3:45 PM Staff were late at attending. Dr. Bloom presided. For 66 days we were not required to openly give out our names in order to speak at the Community Meeting. Dr. Bloom said if we wanted to participate in the meeting we had to say our name. I asked Dr. Bloom if he was "dictating policy at will" and he said yes. As I said this was previously not required. I believe his actions to be debilitating; Dr. Bloom thinks the above to be therapeutic of which I don't believe. I think the opposite.

R.1. Dr. Bloom (2-20-91):

At breakfast Dr. Bloom came into the cafeteria and went over to a Ed (patient). In front of everyone, loud and clear, Dr. Bloom asked Ed if he had his bowel movement. Now, ask yourself, if you were in a group of people and someone came up to you and asked you (in front of everyone) if you had your bowel movement yet, wouldn't you be embarrassed? I feel this to be unprofessional, non-therapeutic, ignorant, and uncurtious. The Doctor could have pulled Ed aside and quietly settled the matter diplomatically.

S. Dr. Rank – Psychiatrist – (12-12-90):

Via Community Meeting Dr. Rank (Speaker); she did not know there is a Rights of Inpatients in Psychiatric Centers of The NYS Office of Mental Health Handbook as is posted in the Gameroom display board. It is one of two Handbooks displayed and per Forensic Unit Patient Handbook it states on page 11 that I'm supposed to receive such a Handbook upon Admission. Today was the first day I received a Handbook and made aware of its being. This was a clear violation of policy.

S.1. Dr. Rank (2-28-91):

I said to Dr. Rank that I would like to ask a question concerning movies and would like her response. I said that movies are being shown pretty much all day and night (on the weekends) on the one side of the Dayroom. It also happens on weekdays, day and night. I said lately, like the last two weeks, movies have been shown during the day as well (i.e. on weekdays). I also said the TV is turned on the other side of the room (at designated times). My question addressed to Dr. Rank (P.H.D.) was, "Does she think this to be therapeutic?" She answered, " Well, I have to discuss it with the Team to find out the number of times movies have been played to see if it is therapeutic." My point was the frequency and the simple question of being therapeutic. Based on several attempts, I never got an answer.

S.2. Dr. Rank (4-04-91):

Dr. Rank started a patient (Chris) on an activity (Learning the computer) before 9:30 AM (i.e. 9:00 AM). This goes against policy per page 20 of The Forensic Unit Handbook. The Handbook states, "For the most part, activities are available for patients to attend between 9:30 – 11:30 AM."

T. Cat – Recreational Therapist (5-06-91):

Cat presiding, at a Community Meeting from 11:35 - 11:55 AM, I brought up that there are no written grievance procedures for the Forensic Unit. For the most part, people concurred with me that there should be a written grievance procedure. This is an Internal Control Weakness for one thing, Staff are able to dictate policy at their own will with no formal system for patient refute or possible patient recompense (there was no audit or paper trail). I subsequently gave the Hospital Director a written draft grievance procedure for the Forensic Unit. I never heard any final response back from these people and during my stay at the Forensic Unit a written grievance procedure was never instituted.

U. Staff (In General) (1-17-91):

While eating breakfast, Staff brought the TV into the Dining Room to watch the news concerning the Iraq War. We had no choice to watch this whether or not we wanted to watch. My point here is that we always have the choice of watching the news from 9:00 - 9:30 AM in the Day Room and also have access to the newspaper if we want to read it. Staff, however, overlooked that everyone may not have wanted to see or hear the TV news let alone during the breakfast hour. Staff did not ask or address such a question to the group. This represents another situation of lack of Internal Control and ultimately buffoonery.

U.1. Staff (In General) (1-21-91):

The Dayroom and Recreationroom was left unattended for at least five minutes. I was told this Forensic Unit was a Maximum Security Housing which housed even murderers and violent people. This is another situation of a lack of Internal Control.

U.2. Staff (In General) (1-21-91):

Official Deputys are rarely seen in the Dayroom or Recreation room. They only usually appear in these Rooms periodically and only for a few minutes. Sometimes a fight or turbulence breaks out. There are, for the most part, Ladies (Aides) that oversee operations in the Dayroom, and, Recreationroom, etc.. I believe Ladies can't handle and are not equipped to handle these dangerous matters. Point noted, there are even murderers in this facility. Again, without constant surveillance of Deputys, these Ladies are not physically equipped to handle these so called, Mentally Ill and Dangerous patients (a danger to themselves or others).

U.3. Staff (In General) (1-29-91):

Harold (patient) did not want to go to the Church Service. Harold kept saying that he did not want to be at this church service and Harold almost hit the Pastor. In my opinion, no one should be forced to go to a religious service. Per Rights of Inpatients Handbook page 3, it says, under personal rights we have the Right to "Practice of the religion of your choice"; which includes NO CHOICE. Idiots.

U.4. Staff (In General) (2-02-91):

With parents, patients, and Staff in the Visitingroom the air was filled with cigarette smoke. This Visitingroom is not a designated smoking area. Per Ms. Bider (Aide), it is against the Law to smoke in any Non designated smoking areas.

U.5. Staff (In General) (2-02-91):
Concerning Patients, Harold, Robert, Ed, etc.; Staff let patients stay up virtually all hours of the night and let patients pace in the Dormroom back and forth. This pacing makes it hard for others to get to sleep and stay asleep. I'm surprised Staff does not keep them stationary as they do during the nap hours. I, in fact, had these so-called "Pacers" stumble across the end of my bed and wake me up at night.

U.6. Staff (In General) (2-19-91):
The Travel Club met in the Recreationroom with an audiovisual film and left the door open to the Dayroom. We can be either in the one of these two rooms. Cat (Recreation Therapist), Ms. Brent (Aide), and Ms. Haw (Aide) are all present in the Dayroom and do not close the Recreationroom door. As Cat knows, this is one of her treatment activities. I sure did not want to be in any part of any treatment activity in any way, shape, or form (at least at this period of time). Everybody in the Dayroom had to listen to their travel movie whether they wanted to or not. Staff could have easily closed the Recreationroom door; just another Internal Control weakness. The patients, here, have the right to refuse any form of Treatment per Rights of Inpatients Handbook.

U.7. Staff (In General) (2-23-91):
Another quagmire; some of the larger heating units located in the Dayroom, Recreationroom, Cafeteria, and Dormrooms are so hot you can get burned if you touch them. There are no warning signs to caution you not to touch these heating units.

U.8. Staff (In General) (2-25-91):
Staff, including Cat (Recreation Therapist), gave Harold (patient) a needle to sew up his sweater at the elbow areas. Harold was doing this in the Dayroom in the presence of patients on level one and two, (which are the least privileged patients), etc.. To top this, no Aide was near Harold to Supervise him. I believe this to be contraband (i.e. needles), especially in the presence of a believed to be mentally ill and either a danger to themselves or others. There are mostly Men patients and mostly Women Aides whereby these Men could easily overpower/overcome the Women Aides; included in the Forensic Unit were Men Murderers. These needles could have been easily overpowered from Harold and used as a deadly weapon. Per page 9 of the Forensic Unit Handbook states, Contraband includes any items that could be used to inflict injury on another person. The Handbook goes on to say "the security rules of the RRFU may at times seem strict and burdensome. However, if one substitutes the

word "safety" for the word "security", the rules may be easier to understand. The safety of all Patients, Staff members, and Visitors is a primary concern to the Unit Administrators." Another note is that there were no Deputys present. This could have proved to be a serious and a grave situation for everyone. What are Staff thinking?

U.9. Staff (In General) (3-18-91):

Staff allowed a Joanne (patient) to wear her nighty (pajamas or pullover type) in the Dayroom among 16 Men who are supposedly mentally ill and dangerous. What kind of discretion is this? This is poor judgement on Staffs part; stupidity.

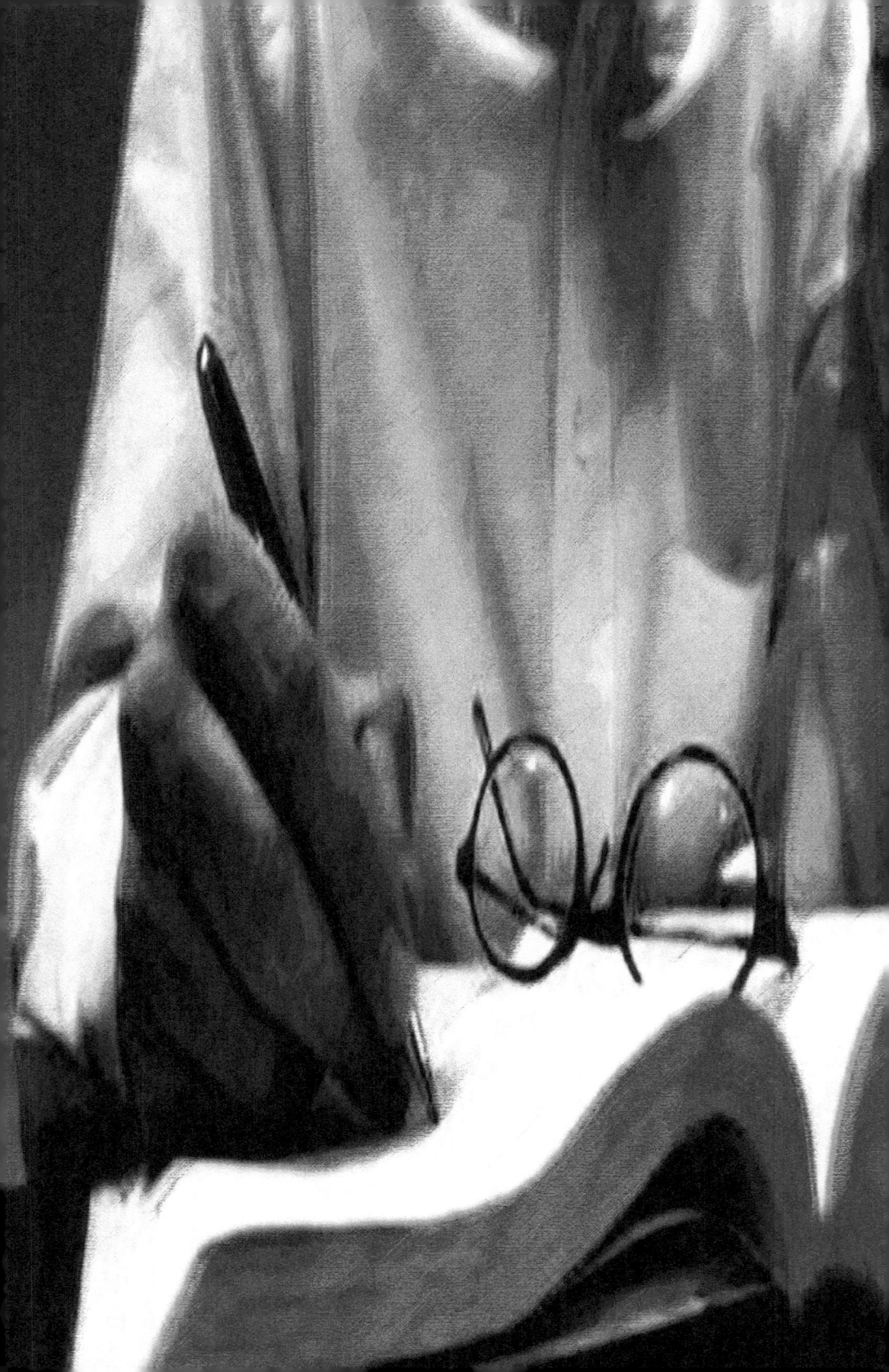

CHAPTER 9

Workman's Compensation Hearing Letter
Per Decision of the Hearing Representative
And Also My Additional Insight Per This Letter
Hearing Was Held On February 28, 1996 In
Buffalo, New York
Another Great Satan System

By Mark C. Russell

The following pages are verbatim (Letter) of the Hearing Representative's Decision Concerning My Not Getting Workman's Compensation:

U. S. DEPARTMENT OF LABOR

Office of Worker's Compensation Programs

DECISION OF THE HEARING REPRESENTATIVE

In the matter of the claim is whether the claimant sustained an emotional condition arising in the performance of his duties.

The claimant, born March 21, 1961, is an employee of the U. S. Department of Defense. On September 7, 1994, he filed a Notice of Occupational Injury and Claim for Compensation alleging that he sustained a paranoia condition while in the performance of his duties. He advised that he worked in a top secret position and the information and environment of his job caused him to seek psychiatric help.

The evidence shows that the claimant was employed with the Department of Defense from January of 1986 through July of 1989. During the early part of this period of time, the claimant worked in a top secret position. He explained that it was not position itself that caused his paranoia, but the top secret environment. He stated that everyone was very serious about security, and his privacy was invaded to insure that security was upheld. He was told that his phone was tapped and cameras were installed in his home to spy on him. The claimant received an admonishment for breach of security for an event occurring on February 20, 1987. In a memorandum dated April 21,1987, from Steve, Branch Manager, the claimant was advised of the security violation and was reminded of his responsibility in this regard. Steve told the claimant that if he was unsure of the appropriate procedures, that he should inquire. The claimant responded to Steve, noting that there are no established procedures for document security, and while he would be more careful in the future, he felt that preventative measures should be taken by Management. The claimant also provided information noting that investigations revealed inadequate supervision and security omissions in the office where the claimant worked.

The claimant gave names of his co-workers and advised of conversations he had with these individuals concerning security and things he was told about his apartment being bugged and his every move being seen. There was only one individual who provided a statement concerning the events that occurred. Mr. Davide, noted that he was serving as Acting Branch Manager when the claimant was employed as a Junior Auditor. He noted the claimant's job duties, and indicated that the office was a secure environment. Mr. Davide indicated that the claimant was expected to comply with security procedures, such as proper safeguarding of classified documents; ensuring discussion of classified information was with appropriate individuals; and end-of-day lockup. He noted that he could not confirm or dispute the claimant's allegations of being spied on or that someone broke into his apartment. Mr. Davide noted that the claimant was adamant that these things were happening, and he tried to assure him that no one in the office would do what he was alleging. The claimant accused Mr. Davide of being involved, and he indicated that he reported the issue to his supervisors. The claimant shortly thereafter left on extended leave and then was transferred.

The file contains medical reports noting that the claimant was being treated for Paranoia 297.10 in DSM III. Dr. Michael P. provided a report dated January 13, 1995, referring to his previous reports and specific findings. He noted that there may be a genetic component to the claimant illness with family history reported, but that the claimant was 100 percent convinced that he was being driven crazy by his job environment and that the government was capable of doing this. Dr. P. stated, "I cannot state that I believe his paranoia is directly causatively due to the events as he described them (numerous contacts with Coworkers who related to him the technology capable of the government, that they were possibly breaking into his apartment and spying on him, etc.) without confirmation of this occurrence from these individuals or by alternative means. If these were proven to be true, then yes, I would say that this disabling condition of paranoia is due to the events that occurred on the job. However, given the nature in which security needs to be strictly adhered to in the kind of environment he worked in, which paid a great deal of attention to security and the ability to spy, etc., it is my belief that his condition was aggravated by the type of employment that he was engaged in as an accountant for Defense Contract Auditing."

The Office noted specific conversations and events as alleged by the claimant in the Memorandum to the Director dated August 10, 1995, indicating there was no documentation to support that these conversations and events actually occurred. The Office advised the claimant of the denial of his claim as the evidence failed to establish that an injury was sustained as alleged. The claimant disagreed with that decision and requested an oral hearing.

At the hearing, the claimant testified as to how he believed his paranoia condition was causally related to his work environment. Again, the claimant stressed that he felt that it was the environment in which he worked, not his job, that caused his condition. He explained that security was constantly stressed. Each day when he came to work, he had to show a badge, and then be let in through locked doors, into an area with no windows or access other than the locked doors. He had a combination to drawers in which he would place his work each night. He was shown movies on security and was told by his supervisors and co-workers that his phones could be bugged and his apartment could be wired so that the government could spy on him at all times to ensure that security was not broken. The claimant explained that the Inspector General investigated his office, and found that there was insufficient supervision and lack of procedures for security measures. While security was stressed, the claimant did not feel adequately prepared to meet his responsibilities in this regard. He stated that he was admonished at one point for a security violation.

Regarding whether he could substantiate the fact that his co-workers harassed him about bugging and spying by the government, the claimant advised that there was no one left there that he could call on for a statement. Even if there were, he was sure that no one would admit to what has transpired at that time. While Mr. Davide advised in his statement that he could not recall any of the events, the claimant indicated that this was a lie as Mr. Davide had told him many of the things himself. He felt that Mr. Davide was protecting himself and his job by making the statement that he did.

The claimant submitted an additional medical report from Dr. Angela H., dated May 12,1995, Dr. H. reported on her evaluation of the claimant, and that his problems began in 1987 when he was working for a top secret government agency, requiring a high degree of security precautions. She indicated that the claimant reported of conversations he had with his supervisor and co-workers, concerning employees being watched by hidden cameras and microphones. He stated that his supervisor told him he was being spied on at home, and co-workers told him his apartment was searched. He was told to be careful of his working environment and his belief that he was being watched and monitored caused his functioning to deteriorate. Dr. H. stated, "He continued to feel harassed by his former employer and was frustrated by their denial that there was anything amiss in his work environment that caused his condition and frustration by the lack of channels for redress. It was in this state of mind that he broke a car windshield at a car dealership because he wanted to draw attention to his plight and be able to tell his story in court. This resulted in an admission to Rochester Psychiatric Center Forensic Unit from 9-13-90 to 10-13-90. However, he was readmitted after he burned a neighbor's shed for the same reasons and stayed from 12-11-90 to 4-93. Dr. H. opined, "In my opinion, Mr. Russell had an emotional breakdown precipitated by the working conditions and specific incidents at the D.C.A.A. His diagnosis remains Delusional Disorder, paranoid type."

Workers' compensation law does not apply to each and every injury or illness that is somehow related to an individual's job. There are situations where an injury or illness has some connection with the employment but does not come within the coverage of the Federal Employees' Compensation Act. These injuries occur in the course of employment and have the same kind of causal connection with it but are not covered because they are found not to have risen out of the employment. Where disability results from an employee's emotional reaction to his regular or specially assigned duties, coverage may be afforded under the act. (1)

The claimant has specifically indicated both in writing and in his oral testimony that his paranoia condition was not due to his position or the work that he performed but to the environment in which he worked. He advised that the position was in a top security location and that security was constantly stressed. While the claimant did testify that he had to show a badge and secure documents every night, the main point brought out in the file is that he was becoming overwhelmed with conversations he alleged transpired between himself and his supervisor and co-workers. He stated that he was repeatedly told of bugging devices and being spied on and watched at every turn.

For harassment to give rise to a compensable disability under the Act, there must be some evidence that such implicated acts of harassment did, in fact, occur. Mere perceptions of harassment are not compensable. A claimant must substantiate such allegations with probative and reliable evidence. (2)

One piece of evidence the claimant provided is a memorandum following up on an oral admonishment for a security violation. I do not find this to be harassing, but only supporting that security was a vital issue, and that assistance could be rendered if procedures were not clear as they involve security measures. There are no statements to support that anyone was bugging the claimant's phones, or breaking into this apartment to plant devices or cameras to spy on him. While the claimant was sincere in his beliefs and the medical documentation from his psychiatrists support that these were his true feelings, there is no probative and reliable evidence to substantiate these conversations as factual. Mr. Davide could not provide any confirmation in this regard.

(1) Debbie Hobbs, Docket NO. 91-0150.
(2) Ruth Borden, Docket NO. 91-915

The claimant's reaction to the security measures required in his position were self- imposed and cannot be considered as a factor of employment arising in the performance of duty.

Accordingly, the Compensation Order issued August 10, 1995, is hereby AFFIRMED.

DATED: 18 April 1996

WASHINGTON, D.C.

Vicki L. S.

Hearing Representative for

Director, Office of

Workers' Compensation Programs

My Additional Insight Per Workman's Compensation Letter Of The Hearing Representative:

Per additional insight, see above Hearing Representative's comments concerning Inter – Office Memorandum (Oral Admonishment – Security Violation dated 4-21-87) and my Grievance Reply (dated 5-19-87); then see Appendix for these two letters for detailed reference. (1) Per Oral Admonishment. Steve (Branch Manager), Steve said I had a subject **"Procedural Noncompliance". Plainly, there were no Procedures.** (2) Steve supposedly told me that if I was unsure of the appropriate Procedures, that I should inquire. With something of this magnitude/importance for security compliance, there should have been Written Procedures. Pointedly, how can I prove that Written Procedures are vital, important, and a necessity concerning the sensitivity of this matter? (A) A G-12 Auditor (my Coworker) who has been there for four years got the same Oral Admonishment (B) Mr. Davide (Acting Branch Manager), himself, decided (on his accord), to put together Written Procedures (concerning Document Destruction) immediately after my Grievance Reply. Mr. Davide even had myself and every one in the office sign off on these **Newly Written Procedures**. Simply, Steve and Mr. Davide were in the wrong. They, themselves should have taken the burden concerning this Oral Admonishment; nobody else.

Per additional insight, Dr. Michael P. (psychiatrist), mentions there may be a genetic component to the claimant illness with family history reported. Yes, I do have an Uncle who has had problems with Paranoia Schizophrenia. But concerning this correlation, I've read NAMI ADVOCATE VOL. 16, NO. 6 with an article called, "Research–Schizophrenia runs in families on page 4 May/June 1995." Per Article, a proposed chart presents the risks of developing Schizophrenia for second – degree (Uncles) relatives of individuals with Schizophrenia. As it clearly points out, genetics play a role, but are not sufficient, to cause Schizophrenia. If you read the chart for Uncles, there is a 2% Lifetime risk of developing Schizophrenia (moot, wouldn't you say?). To also note, even Nephews are at 4% (also moot). I also believe Dr. Michael P. is living in the Dark Ages and is naïve. Dr. P. does not believe that people and employees in my top secret environment may plainly spy; Wake - Up Dr. P. there are many peoples involved. A most noteable case of Government illegalities/improprieties is the ABU GHRAIB IRAQ PRISON SCANDAL, one, of many Government VICIOUS SCANDALS. Dr. P. blindly believes 'security needs to be strictly adhered to in the kind of environment he (myself) worked in, which paid a great deal of attention to security and the ability to spy, etc.'. Dr. P. has no idea what these jerks do. As I pointed out previously the Government is breaking top secret International Law (See Preface explanation on page 12). Does this naïve and stupid Doctor know about this type of thing? I claim not, and, I don't believe Dr. Michael P. has the capacity to make reasoned judgements concerning myself!

As noted in the above Hearing Letter, Mr. Davide (Acting Branch Manager), ' could not recall any of the events'. I had also stated, 'as for the Government subordinates/employees, there was noone left there that I could get a statement from and was sure no subordinate/employee would admit to what has transpired at that time; they could possibly lose their jobs (possibly under life threatening/pressures)'. This is plainly lies on Mr. Davide's part.

Per additional insight, the following is a Memo from Dr. Angela H., M.D. to a Mr. Kill (Attorney). It provides more insight to what Ms. Vicki L. S. (Hearing Representative) wrote concerning Dr. Angela H. (from above Hearing Letter).

Verbatim is the following Memo:

Dr. Angela H., M.D. 5/04/95 Note:
To: Mr. Kill
"I've probably omitted some key information. Instead of obsessing over this anymore, this is what I've put together."
    I didn't mention diagnosis but it would be Delusional Disorder, persecutory type. Of course, this assumes that the things
 Mark says happened, really did not happen, but maybe they did."
Dr. H.

Even Dr. H. is unclear/ not sure of transpired events said did or did not happen. Does this make Dr. Angela H. psychotic? Think about it.
    Per additional insight, Hearing Representative, Ms. Vicki L. S., "there is no probative/ reliable evidence to substantiate these conversations as factual." I have documented over time many of the conversations that went on between purported people and myself. This is reliable competent evidential matter. Again, these people won't admit to their corrupt system, after all, they take two hour lunch breaks, bring to work pornographic movies, have Harold's (Co-worker) Lady Fling calling herself "Love Pool" call the office during work hours, and have constant testing of my religious beliefs (i.e. blasphemous statements, etc.). Ms. Vicki L. S. talks about reliability; how reliable can she call these people as I have described? Vicki is stupid and naïve. How can Ms. Vicki L. S. say the following, "The claimant's reaction to the security measures required in his position were self imposed and can not be considered as a factor of employment arising in the performance of duty." This is totally an injustice, an unreasonableness, a shamefulness, a grievance, an unfairness, a partiality, a one-sidedness, and an inequitableness.
    A final additional insight, just by reading this Letter, in and of itself, can you come to the conclusion that I was the VICTIM; I'm just a little fish in a big pond. I believe there was a bigger injustice by not awarding me Workman's Compensation. In reality, I did not want to afford the insurmountable Attorney fees (i.e. tens of thousands of dollars) to try to properly fight these people. Lastly, I've taken upon myself to write this book.

CHAPTER 10

Lack of Channels For Redress
A Systematic Revelation

By Mark C. Russell

INTRODUCTION:

Dr. Angela H. (psychiatrist) Sets The Tone:

In previous reference of my book (concerning my employment with the Department of Defense/ Defense Contract Audit Agency Government) Dr. Angela H. (Brockport, New York Psychiatrist) said, " He continued to feel harassed by his former employer and was frustrated by their denial that there was anything amiss in his work environment that caused his condition and frustration by the lack of channels for redress."

Various Lack Of Channels For Redress:

The above statement from Dr. Angela H. sets the tone, stage, and atmosphere, of my Government episode concerning "lack of channels for redress". Included are as follows: (1) I conversed with at least four Editors and wrote 2 letters to the Democrat & Chronicle newspaper which all left me void to no avail. (2) I had picketed (with signs, pamphlets, and verbal means) giving away Top Secret Classified information all over Rochester, New York including the front door of the downtown Rochester D & C newspaper (to no avail-no arrest). (3) I contacted several Rochester Attorneys (for a Civil Suit, etc.) but they said it would cost me tens of thousands of dollars in which to sue the government and many did not know who could specifically represent me which left me to no avail. (4) I contacted, in person, the American Civil Liberties Union (ACLU) to which help was to no avail. (5) I was not awarded Workman's Compensation (see Chapter 9 for details). (6) I've sent my Book Manuscript to the following places: (a) CBS News 60 Minutes, (b) 20/20, (c) Primetime Thursday, (d) Dateline MBC, (e) Montel, (f) OPRAH, (g) The 700 Club, (h) Channels 8,10, & 13. All were "negative" or " no" responses. (7) Democrat &Chronicle Essays for Speaking Out Piece – sent these essays out for newspaper publishing to no avail. (8) The Government itself, underhandedly, never did a viable/reliable investigation; in effect, my Government episode was swept under the rug. Pointedly, I could not find anybody to help my situation of redress.

The following expands upon or details the above numbers (1) through (8):

1   Newspaper Editors: The following are contact Editors of the Democrat & Chronicle (D&C) newspaper of which I tried (to no avail) to get them to print a story herein:

EDITOR #1 1-30-90 at 1:25-2:30 PM – I met this Editor in person at the D & C. I told this Editor that a Naval Investigative Service Agent (NIS) was informed, in person (myself), that I gave away Top Secret information to my Psychiatric Therapist. On 1-31-90 at 10:30 AM, the same newspaper and Editor as above, this Editor was informed by the FBI and NIS that the classified information given to my Therapist was not as serious as it could have been. The FBI also told the Editor that I was on Disability. The Editor told me he would not write a story because he felt he did not have enough information and background. I told him that the NIS Agent said I did commit a crime and that they were not going to arrest me for it. What more do you need for a story?

EDITOR #2 3-06-90 at 2:00 PM – I talked through the lobby phone at the D & C. This Editor was from the Assignment Area. I told this Editor that my story was important and that it could make him "President". This Editor said he had no ambition to become President. This Editor wanted more information over the phone but I told him it was private and that people were standing around me. He said people don't care but I said yes, they do. The next day on 3-07-90 at 1:00 PM again on the Lobby phone, I talked to this same Editor for approximately 20 minutes. This Editor did not think there was a story because I did not tell him why I did this and that he was going to wait for any action, if any, by the authorities. I told this Editor I could give him names of Authorities I talked with from the FBI & NIS but he would not have anything to do with them. He would not even let me to go upstairs to discuss in private with a reporter the details. I told this Editor I didn't want to discuss this over the phone when there were several people standing around me. I did not think this to be proper but he said that these people don't care but I disagreed. Anyway, I did not meet privately. I did however said I had committed a crime but nothing was done and that this is what the story would be based on. And, obviously this Editor just ditched me.

EDITOR #3 3-07-00 – I wrote and sent out a letter to this Editor as of this date. This letter included information found in chapters 1 & 2 of my book. I never received a response back.

EDITOR #4 5-31-02 – I wrote and sent out a letter to this Editor as of this date. I invited this Editor to my Court hearing in the Town of Ogden on 6-26-02 at 5:00 PM. I informed her extensively concerning my Top Secret Government episode. I never received a response from her.

2 The following are places, dates, and times I went to giving away Top Secret classified information by means of posters, mouth, post-its, and/or pamphlets (i.e. refer to Preface Page 12 – last paragraph; to no avail-no arrest was made):

By Mark C. Russell

DATE	TIME	LOCATION
2-06-90	—	Chase Pitkins
2-07-90	2:00-4:00 PM	RIT
2-08-90	1:45-3:30 PM	SUNY Brockport College
2-09-90	1:30-2:30 PM	U. of Rochester
2-12-90	1:00-4:00 PM	SUNY Brockport College
2-13-90	2:00-5:00 PM	RIT
2-14-90	1:30-2:30 PM	U. of Rochester
2-26-90	2:00-4:00 PM	Wegmans, FAYS, Logos, & Bells
2-27-90	1:30-4:00 PM	Freddy's & Marketplace Mall

You may ask yourself; why did I do this? Well, because there was no viable investigation, during my Government employment, into improprieties/illegalities and lack of channels for redress thereof. As noted, the Government knows very well what I've been doing; my every move (i.e. this is illegal of course).

VARIOUS BANK REPRESENTATIVES WERE GIVEN TOP SECRET INFORMATION:

3-12-90   3:00 PM
First National Bank, N.A.
2147 West Ridge Road
Rochester, NY 14626

3-19-90   2:00 PM
Norstar Bank, N.A.
Westgate Office
1948 Chili Avenue
Rochester, NY 14624

3-19-90   2:45 PM
Chase Lincoln First Bank, N. A.
Rochester Division, Gates Office
6 Spencerport Road
Rochester, NY 14606

3-20-90   1:55 PM
Columbia Banking
Fed., Savings, & Loan Assoc.
4871 Lake Road South
Brockport, NY 14420

3-20-90   2:15 PM
First Federal-Savings & Loan
Assoc. of Rochester
Brockport Office
4771 South Lake Road
Brockport, NY 14420-2453

3-23-90   1:30 PM
First National Bank of Rochester
1370 Lyell Avenue
Rochester, NY 14606

3-26-90   12:15 PM
Marine Midland Bank, N. A.
184 South Unior Street
Spencerport, NY 14559
Rochester, NY 14624

3-26-90   1:10 PM
Key Bank
A Key Corp. Bank
Stoneridge Office
Rochester, NY 14615

3-26-90   2:15 PM
Chase Lincoln First Bank, N.A.
Irondequoit East Ridge Road
Rochester, NY 14622

3-26-90   2:45 PM
Citicorp Citi Bank
2255 Ridge Road East
Rochester, NY 14622

3-27-90   1:05 PM
First Federal Savings & Loan
Assoc. of Rochester
Henrietta Office

1100 Jefferson Road
Rochester, NY 14623
3-27-90   1:50 PM
Columbia Banking
Federal Savings & Loan Assoc.

3-23-90   1:15 PM

Central Trust
Lyell Office
1385 Lyell Avenue
Rochester, NY 14606

3-23-90   1:55 PM
Citicorp Citibank
1955 Buffalo Road
Rochester, NY 14624

3-26-90   12:40 PM
Columbia Banking
Federal Savings & Loan Assoc.
1975 Buffalo Road

3-26-90   1:45 PM
Citicorp, Citibank
424 Ridge Road West
Rochester, NY 14615

3-26-90   2:20 PM
Marine Midland Bank, N.A.
2255 Ridge Road West
Rochester, NY 14622

3-27-90   12:55 PM
Chase Lincoln First Bank, N.A.
Henrietta Office
1575 East Henrietta Road
Rochester, NY 14623

3-27-90   1:20 PM
Marine Midland Bank, N.A.
3301 Winton Road South

Rochester, NY 14623

3-27-90   2:15 PM
Central Trust
Pittsford Office

By Mark C. Russell

3420 Monroe Avenue   3290 Monroe Avenue
Rochester, NY 14618   Rochester, NY 14618

3-27-90   2:30 PM
First Federal Savings & Loan
Assoc. Of Rochester
3195 Monroe Avenue
Rochester, NY 14618

The following is an extension of Number (2) above. It includes places, dates, and times I gave away Top Secret classified information by means of posters, mouth, post-its, and or pamphlets as follows:

DATE	TIME	LOCATION
4-02-90	1:10 PM	K&K Foodmart Brockport (woman)
4-02-90	1:20 PM	K&K Foodmart Brockport (man)
4-02-90	1:30 PM	Fays Drug Brockport (woman)
4-02-90	1:40 PM	Huey's Deli & Dairy Brockport (woman)
4-02-90	2:00 PM	Hook's Farm MKT. Rt. 31 (woman)
4-02-90	2:15 PM	Town Club RT.31 Near Modex (woman)
4-02-90	2:50 Pm	Red Carpet Deli & Pizzeria Lomb Drive-near RIT (woman)
4-02-90	3:20 PM	Mobile Gas Corner Howard & Buffalo (woman)
4-03-90	1:20 PM	Mobile Parma Corners (woman)
4-03-90	1:30 PM	84 Lumber Ridge Road (man)
4-03-90	1:35 PM	Getty Gas Elmgrove & Ridge
4-03-90	2:20 PM	Goodyear Ridge & Nantucket
4-03-90	2:30 PM	Moran's Paint & Wallpaper Greece

This is a continuation of above number (2). It includes dates, times, and places giving away Top Secret information of various means as follows:

DATE	TIME	LOCATION	
4-03-90	2:35 PM	Nick's Drycleaners Greece	
4-03-90	2:45 PM	Minimart Greece	
4-03-90	2:46 PM	Mobile Longridge Mall	
4-03-90	2:55 PM	Century 21 Buckman's Center	
4-03-90	2:57 PM	Housework's Buckman's Center	
4-03-90	3:00 PM	Empire Electric Greece	
4-03-90	3:05 PM	Cerimi's Pizza Ridge Road	
4-03-90	3:15 PM	Rosa & Sullivan Ridge Road	
4-03-90	3:20 PM	Convient Farms Food Mart Ridge Rd.	
4-03-90	3:25 PM	C & C Motors Ridge Rd.	
4-04-90	3:35 PM	Peterson's Drugs	
4-06-90	2:20 PM	Buffalo Road Plaza	(man)
4-06-90	2:22 PM	"	(man)
4-06-90	2:25 PM	"	(woman)
4-06-90	2:28 PM	"	"
4-06-90	2:30 PM	"	"
4-06-90	2:40 PM	"	"
4-06-90	3:00 PM	"	"

By Mark C. Russell

DATE	TIME	LOCATION	
4-06-90	3:05 PM	"	(man)
4-06-90	3:15 PM	"	(man)
4-06-90	3:20 PM	"	(woman)
4-07-90	1:00 PM	Long Ridge Mall - Time Out	
4-07-90	1:30 PM	"	Rite Aid Pharmacy
4-07-90	1:35 PM	"	Middle Mall Stand
4-07-90	1:45 PM	"	The Gap
4-07-90	2:00 PM	"	Stand near Marjax's
4-07-90	2:05 PM	"	T. J. Cinnamons Bakery
4-07-90	2:20 PM	"	McCurdy's (upstairs)

This is a continuation of above Number (2). It includes dates, times, and places giving away Top Secret information as follows:

DATE	TIME	LOCATION
4-07-90	2:30 PM	LongRidge Mall – Marjax's
4-07-90	2:45 PM	" Things Remembered
4-07-90	3:15 PM	Station Break – GreeceTown Mall
4-07-90	4:00 PM	McDonald's – LongRidge Mall
4-08-90	1:30 PM	Peterson's Drugs Slocum Rd. Ontario
4-09-90	12:45 PM	Wegman's Ridgemont
4-09-90	1:15 PM	KMART Ridgemont

DATE	TIME	LOCATION
4-09-90	2:00 PM	Sugar Creek Gas Bergen RT. 33
4-09-90	2:10 PM	Gulf Gas "
4-09-90	2:15 PM	James Sullivan AgencyCorner RT. 33 & 19
4-09-90	2:20 PM	Napa (Bergen)
4-09-90	2:35 PM	A touch of Country Class (Churchville)
4-09-90	3:15 PM	LongRidge Information
4-09-90	3:20 PM	" Waldens
4-09-90	3:25 PM	" Woolworth's
4-09-90	3:30 PM	" Foot Locker
4-05-90	11:00 AM	Wegmans Chili Rd.
4-10-90	1:15 PM	RIT Placement Receptionist
4-10-90	2:45 PM	Hallmark Rochester Downtown Mall
4-10-90	3:00 PM	Rite Aid "
4-10-90	3:25 PM	Foot Locker "
4-10-90	3:25 PM	Clinton Ave. Parking Garage Attendant
4-11-90	1:35 PM	Town Club Spencerport
4-13-90	1:20 PM	Peir 1 Imports, Toys "R" US, Wegmans MKT. Place Mall, T-Shirt
4-13-90	2:30 PM	Empire Electric, Wegmans, Greece Town Mall "
4-14-90	12:20 PM	Federal Bldg. "

DATE	TIME	LOCATION
4-14-90	12:35 PM	Gannett Newspaper "
4-14-90	12:40-2:00 PM	Downtown Rochester Mall "

This is a continuation of above Number (2). It includes dates, times, and places giving away Top Secret information as follows:

DATE	TIME	LOCATION
4-14-90	2:30-4:00 PM	Pittsford Plaza T-Shirt
4-14-90	7:00-8:00 PM	Irondequoit Mall "
4-15-90	7:30 AM	(man)
4-16-90	1:10 PM	Spencerport P.O. (man)
4-17-90	9:30 AM	Goodyear
4-17-90	2:20 PM	Longridge Mall Info. Desk
4-17-90	3:05 PM	Logos Bookstore
4-18-90	3:00 PM	Brockport Library
4-20-90	2:00 PM	U. of Rochester 1rst Floor desk person
4-20-90	4:00 PM	Carmines 3 Woman at counter
4-22-90	10:00 AM	Bible Class
4-22-90	3:00 PM	Longridge Woolworth's
4-22-90	3:15 PM	GreeceTown Mall
4-22-90	3:30 PM	Fed. Bldg. & Times Union

DATE	TIME	LOCATION
4-23-90	2:00-3:30 PM	Brockport College Poster
4-24-90	11:20 AM	Bells Spencerport Woman
4-25-90	2:00-4:15 PM	Times Union Poster
5-02-90	?	Misc. Places
5-02-90	3:00 PM	U. of Rochester Library Desk Person
5-08-90	11:30-2:30 PM	Gannett New, Fed. Bldg.
5-09-90	3:30-5:30 PM	E. Henrietta Rd. & Westfall Rd.
5-10-90	3:00 PM	U. of Rochesterr Library 3rd fl. (mouth)
5-12-90	12:00-1:30 PM	Federal Bldg. (posters)
5-14-90	1:30-4:00 PM	Gannett Newspaper (posters)
5-15-90	1:45-3:30 PM	Corner Jefferson & E. Henrietta Rd. (posters)
5-15-90	6:10 PM	A Plus Mini Market Spencerport (mouth)
5-15-90	6:30 PM	Georges Shop Spencerport (mouth)
5-16-90	3:00 PM	Town Hall Henrietta (mouth)

This is a continuation of above Number (2). It includes dates, times, and places giving away Top Secret information as follows:

DATE	TIME	LOCATION
5-16-90	3:05 PM	Town Hall Henrietta –State Police
5-16-90	7:15 PM	LongRidge Two Security Guards (mouth)
5-16-90	7:20 PM	" Rite Aid Drug Store

By Mark C. Russell

DATE	TIME	LOCATION
5-17-90	4:45 PM	Brockport College Library
5-22-90	11:45 AM	Georges Spencerport (mouth)
6-14-90	1:00 PM	Times Union, D & C, & Federal Bldg.
6-16-90	1:00-4:15 PM	Marketplace Mall Entrance
6-19-90	12:30-1:00 PM	Longridge Mall
6-19-90	4:00-6:00 PM	"
6-20-90	3:45-5:45 PM	E. Henrietta & Jefferson Rd. Corner
6-22-90	3:00-5:00 PM	Corner Long Pond & W. Ridge Rd.
6-23-90	1:30-4:00 PM	Corner Wegmans & W. Ridge Rd.
6-23-90	6:45 PM	"
6-24-90	12:30 PM	"
7-10-90	2:00-5:30 PM	Hall of Justice Front Grounds
7-14-90	12:30-4:15 PM	Gannett News (Front)
7-16-90	1:00-2:30 PM	Federal Bldg.
7-16-90	2:30-5:45 PM	Hall of Justice
7-17-90	12:30-5:30 PM	Federal Bldg., Gannett Bldg., Rochester Public Library
7-18-90	12:30-3:45 PM	Corner Platt St. & State St.
7-19-90	2:30-3:00 PM	Greece Town Hall
7-24-90	12:00-5:00 PM	Front Kodak on State St.

DATE	TIME	LOCATION
7-25-90	2:00-5:45 PM	"
7-26-90	1:00-5:30 PM	Rt. 104 Sidewalk (Wegmans)
7-27-90	12:30-5:30 PM	Wegmans Long Pond Rd.
7-28-90	1:45-3:45 PM	Rt. 104 Buckmans
7-30-90	11:00-5:30 PM	Major Charles Carroll Plaza Park
8-02-90	1:15-5:15 PM	GroundRound Westmar Plaza

This is a continuation of above Number (2). It includes dates, times, and places giving away Top Secret information as follows:

DATE	TIME	LOCATION
8-03-90	1:30-5:45 PM	Chili Public Library
8-04-90	1:15-3:30 PM	Greece Town Hall
8-08-90	1:10-5:20 PM	Long Pond & Ridge Rd.
8-09-90	12:30-5:00 PM	City of Rochester
8-10-90	1:30-5:30 PM	"
8-12-90	1:00-4:45 PM	Wegmans Plaza Scottsville
8-14-90	6:45-8:39 PM	Brockport TLRd.
8-15-90	6:30-8:30 PM	N. Manitou Rd.
8-18-90	11:00-2:00 PM	Wegmans & Redman Rd.
8-20-90	6:15-8:15 PM	Sweden Walker Rd.
8-21-90	6:30-8:30 PM	S. Holley Rd.

DATE	TIME	LOCATION
8-22-90	6:20-8:20 PM	Kendale Rd.
8-23-90	6:15-8:30 PM	Jerico Rd. & W. Sweden Rd.
8-24-90	6:15-8:00 PM	W. Bergen Rd.
9-02-90	9:30 Service	Trinity Lutheran Church

3   **Attorneys to help me get arrested** – The following six Attorneys I confided in which to force the FBI to arrest me for giving out classified information; it's a crime. There was little help or direction as I point out for each Attorney which, in essence, is another **"lack of channels for redress"**. Why did I seek this? Because I wanted to expose the Government of their illegal activities, but, in a CourtRoom Setting.

a   **Frank**   6-05-90   11:00 AM
Frank came to the conclusion that I needed a lawyer that does Civil Lawsuits against the Federal Government. He just could not specifically help me.

b   **Mary Anne**   6-05-90   11:45 AM
Mary Anne said I did not need a Civil Type Lawyer which is just the opposite what Frank above said. She said she did not know who I should go to but mentioned the U.S. Attorney of which I found out is exactly wrong. Again, I wanted to take action against the Federal Government; I was not helped.

c   **Anne**   6-05-90   1:45 PM
Anne said that the U.S. Attorneys only handles the Government who gets sued, not people who want to sue the Government. Anne recommended that I call various Lawyers to see if they would take my case, and possibly, see the Lawyer Referral Service. Again, not much help; I've been down this route before with not much help.

d   **Jim**   6-06-90   2:45 PM
Jim (Trial Lawyer) wanted a retainer of $5,000.00. I could not afford him so he mentioned Volunteer Legal Services Project. I went to the Volunteer Legal Services and they said they only do Family Law & some other matters. Volunteer Legal Services said they had no idea who to go to to take action against the Federal Government except Monroe County Bar Association; another dead end.

e **William** 6-06-90   2:55 PM

Again, I wanted the Government (FBI) to arrest me for giving out classified information. Among others, William also led me to Volunteer Legal Services Project which could not help me. William said he did not know what kind or type of Lawyer I would need to prosecute the FBI to do their job; which was to arrest me.

f **Ester** 6-07-90   1:15 PM

Ester was told I wanted the FBI be forced to arrest me for giving out classified information; enforce the law for a crime. She suggestec a Private Attorney. Again, not much help.

To show how expensive a Civil Government suit related Attorney costs I contacted the following Attorneys with a "ball park" estimate/expense per six Attorneys; it's beyond affordable. This represents another lack of channels for redress; as you can see, this type of thing becomes insurmountable:

ATTORNEY	DATE	TIME	COST
Peter	5-10-00	2:00-2:45 PM	Expensive
David	5-15-00	8:30 AM	>$5,000.00
Brian	5-17-00	3:30 PM	$10,000.00
Joseph	5-18-00	9:00 AM	>$5,000.00
John	8-21-00	11:00-12:00 PM	$10,000.00
Mark	5-19-00	3:00 PM	Expensive
Berny	8-16-00	12:15 PM	>$5,000.00

4 American Civil Liberties Union (ACLU) – here I'm only seeking advice concerning First Amendment Rights from the ACLU. As you will see this represents another form of Lack Of Channels For Redress:

a **Kevin (clerical type volunteer – ACLU):** some background information is that I tried to contact someone at the ACLU located at 121 N. Fitzhugh, Rochester, NY on 6-08-90 @ 10:00 AM and called later that day; and 6-08-90 @ 11:15 AM & 3:10 PM (to no avail). Also, on 6-11-90 @ 1:15 PM (to no avail). To avail, on 6-12-90 @ 9:40 AM per ACLU, Kevin, said the ACLU only had a Paralegal working for them because the prior Attorney went into Private Practice. Kevin told me I could wear a picket sign as long as it was not on private property. This clerical worker said if I need a real Attorney to go to the Legal Aid Society, but he did not know if they could help; but I could not wait to ask Bob, their Paralegal, questions. Kevin said I may have to go to an outside Attorney. I did not speak to Bob as of yet.

b   **Bob (Paralegal – ACLU):** Later, per Bob, and his understanding of Henrietta Code, he believes that I can wear a sign around town even in a grocery store. If not, people have the right to see code or rule prohibiting as such. Bob would not make a referral to a lawyer (i.e. a specific name) if I needed legal counseling on this matter. It seems that nobody is in a position to get me an Attorney. Plainly, Bob did not know much. Specifically, Bob did not even know what a Public Demonstration was. Bob said the ACLU will have a new Attorney in 3 weeks after not having an Attorney for a month now. This Attorney may or may not be paid.

c   **Liz (ACLU):** On 7-03-90 @ 9:00-9:45 AM I visited the ACLU office with Liz. She works Monday, Wednesday, & Friday @ 8:30 – 3:00 PM. Liz says she does not specialize in the areas of my concern of carrying signs (size), permits (for signs, pamphlets, public speaking), and doing so in public, quasi public, private, and stores & malls etc.. And whether I could go inside a public building and just be silent but hand out printed materials and carry a sign and go to a store parking lot to hand out materials. Liz did not know where to contact organizations that can help me except maybe the newspaper area or TV news. She did however, mention a press release which is subject to censor. She basically could not help me but suggested I go to a big firm. I said to Liz that nobody could help me and that in my case it's unfair and an injustice; Liz concurred. Liz mentioned that I could possibly go to the Head of Special Events Policies & Procedures at the City Hall. This is another instance of the lack of channels for redress.

5   This section concerns a "No Award" For Workman's Compensation – See Chapter 9 for details (4-18-96). This also represents a lack of channels for redress.

6   Book Manuscripts Sent To Viable News Organizations – I had sent out my Book Manuscripts to the following places with a cover letter.

I received either a "negative" response or received no response at all. This just added to my so-called lack of channels for redress. All responses as marked "X" were "negative"." Other dates were plainly "no response".

	Sent	Response		Sent	Response
CBS News 60 Minutes	7-03-97		Dateline NBC	2-18-00	X
524 West 57th Street	12-21-01		30 Rocketfeller Plaza	12-21-01	
New York, NY 10019	5-31-02		Room 510	5-31-02	
	4-27-05		New York, NY 10112	4-27-05	X
20/20	2-18-00	X	Montel	3-09-00	X
147 Columbus Avenue	12-21-01		433 West 53rd Street	12-21-01	
New York, NY 10023	5-31-02		New York, NY 10019	5-31-02	X
	4-27-05			4-27-05	
Primetime Thursday	11-07-97		OPRAH	3-09-00	X
147 Columbus Avenue	12-21-01		P.O. Box 909715	12-21-01	
New York, NY 10023	5-31-02		Chicago, Illinois 60690	5-31-02	
	4-27-05			4-27-05	
Channel 8	12-21-01		The 700 Club	6-09-03	X
201 Humboldt	5-31-02		977 Centerville	4-27-05	X
Street			Turnpike		
Rochester, NY 14610			Virginia Beach, VA		
			23463		
Channel 10	12-21-01		Geraldo Rivera Live	3-09-00	
191 East Avenue	5-31-02		2200 Fletcher Avenue		
Rochester, NY 14604			Fort Lee, NJ 07024		
Channel 13	12-21-01				
4225 West Henrietta	5-31-02				
Rd.					
Rochester, NY 14623					

7   Democrat & Chronicle Essays for Speaking Out Piece –The following represents submitted Essays to the "Speaking Out Piece" section of the Democratic & Chronicle newspaper. I got all negative responses which to me is another lack of channels for redress:

I submitted the following Essays dated 7-18-97, 8-04-97, 8-18-97, and 9-04-97 to the D & C newspaper. These Essays included Top Secret information which can be found on Preface page 12, last paragraph. I received 3 responses out of 4 submissions. Marked on these

3 responses were: (1) "Accepted other letters that expressed opinion better, (2) Other letters accepted express opinion better and (3) They decided that my letter doesn't meet their needs right now."

8 No reliable Government investigation – Plainly, there was no reliable Government investigation concerning my Government episode.

FURTHER LACK OF CHANNELS FOR REDRESS:

Judge David L.:
U.S. District Court
Western District of New York
U.S. Courthouse
100 State Street, Room 2500
Rochester, New York, NY 14614-1324

Per reference to Chapter One (1), "Top Secret Employment With the Defense Contract Audit Agency (DCAA 1986-1989)," I submitted most of Chapter One (1) and other information (19 pages) to Judge David G. L. per referral from Hon. Judge Manley (during my Court Hearing with him on November 2, 2000). Hon. Judge Manley (during my Court Hearing and upon my request) referred me to Judge L. to help me do an investigation per a 19-page support. The investigation has to do with improprieties of Government employment.

Judge Manley (Hall of Justice) told me that Judge L. had jurisdiction to do an investigation and that I should contact Judge L.. Pointedly, the subject was to investigate statements said to me by my Coworkers (at The Defense Contract Audit Agency) as far back as 1987 that effected me both mentally and emotionally.

Judge L. said the following in respect to my letters to him (dated 2-22-99 & 4-26-99) in his letter/response to me (dated 4-28-99): "I advise you that this Court has no power to "investigate" the matters to which you refer. Courts do not conduct investigations. They hear Civil and Criminal trials." Further, Judge L. and the Hon. Judge Manley did not give me any further advice/ action(s) I could take concerning Due Process within my Government episode or plight. WHY? Both Judges are visibly circumventing anything further process on my part. Do you call this Justice? All a part of Satan's System.

Hon. John J. L. (Member of Congress):
2310 Rayburn House Office Building
Washington, D.C., 20515

My Hon. John J. L. letters (concerning a Federal Government investigation) dated 5-25-99, 8-23-99, 9-08-99, 11-01-99, and 12-13-99 contained two proponents of which the Hon. L. only responded to one of the two proponents. He did not respond to the one following proponent included in each inquiry letter as follows: **"Do an investigation on whether my**

Coworkers did say the things that I said they did" (Again, refer to Chapter One for Coworker Statements). I had given the Hon.L. names of contact, contact addresses, and a contact telephone number of my former employer. All said and done there was no response for all my five letter's proponent inquiries as dated/ stated above. Why this glaring omission?

Shamelle N. L.:
U.S. Department of Justice
Of Professional Responsibility
Room 3335
950 Pennsylvania Ave., M.W.
Washington, D.C. 20530

I sent Shamelle N. L. (Program Analyst) a letter and enclosures dated September 18, 2000. Included, were letters to Ms. Janet Reno, Charles E. Schumer, CBS News 60 Minutes and, letters of Invasion of Privacy & Trespass and a pamphlet of Government Persecution. I again, had asked for Shamelle N. L. **to do an investigation of Coworker statements said to me which affected me psychologically and emotionally while working for the Defense Contract Audit Agency (DCAA) from 1986-1989.** Below is her response.

Shamelle N. L. responded (November 8, 2000) that they are 'limited to reviewing allegations of misconduct against Department of Justice Attorneys (DOJ) which relate to their authority to investigate, litigate, or provide legal advice.' She also said 'they find no credible allegations of misconduct against any DOJ attorney or employee, and are taking no action.' In other words, again, I have not found my correct channel for redress. Why no Due Process or proper redress channels; a cover-up possibly? **Again, there was no investigation concerning Coworker statements.**

Robert A. W.:
Legislative Councel Office of Public & Congressional Affairs
U.S. Department of Justice FBI
Washington, D.C. 20535

I sent Robert A. W. a letter (dated 12-26-2000); I included all copies of my correspondence previously sent to Hon. John J. L.. Included, was for Mr. W. to **"do an investigation on whether my Coworkers did say the things I said they did."** This is in reference to my employment with the Federal Government (Defense Contract Audit Agency 1986-89). Refer to Chapter One (1) concerning Coworker statements said to me. See response to this letter, per Mr. Arthur Radford, below.

Mr. Arthur Radford B.:

In response to my above letter (Robert A. W. 12-26-2000) a Mr. Radford B. – Unit Chief Officer of Public & Congressional Affairs, U.S. Department of Justice, FBI, Washington, D.C. 20535 responded to me in light of Robert A. W.'s retirement. Even so, and again, the issue of **"doing an investigation on whether my Coworkers did say the things that I said they did"** while working for the Department of Defense (Defense Contract Audit Agency) **was never addressed**. Refer to Chapter One (1) concerning my Coworkers statements to me. Once again, there was no channel for redress!

In conclusion, to date, I still have not found an avenue of redress. My ambition is to write this book to address the concerns of redress, retribution, compensation, and truth.

CHAPTER 11

Honorable Judge Manley And Probation
And Honorable Judge Moot
Satan At His Best

By Mark C. Russell

JUDGE MANLEY AND PROBATION – INTENSIVE PROBATION – NO REDUCTION TO GENERAL SUPERVISION:

I was charged with Arson 3rd in Monroe County on 10-16-98 for burning down a GAZEBO. On 11-23-99 (3:30 – 4:05 PM) I met with a Mr. Dick Press (Probation Officer) and with a Ms. Joan VanDrake (Probation Supervisor). Per follow-up Memo dated 11-23-99 of this meeting is summarized as follows: Both Dick and Joan told me I was on **Intensive Probation** for the following dates:

1 Feb. – July 1999 – 6 Mos. Report in person 2X per week.
2 Aug. – Oct. 1999 – 3 Mos. Report in person on Tuesday & telephone in on Thursday.
3 Nov. – Jan. 2000 – 3 Mos. Report in person on Tuesday & telephone in on Thursday.

I was told that Intensive Probation is basically meeting in person at least two times per week for a minimum of six months and maybe up to 11/2 years. Regular Probation or General Supervision is meeting in person a minimum of once per month to a maximum of 4X per month (i.e. maximum of one time per week). Initially, Dick Press, if I did well pertaining to number (3) above (i.e. Nov. – Jan. 2000) I would (if I was doing well on Probation) go on to General Supervision or Regular Probation from Intensive Probation. Subsequently, Dick Press (Probation Officer) told me I was going to be on Intensive Probation (not General Supervision as discussed prior) per our meeting to once per week with a telephone call (i.e. Again, this is different from what he told me prior). Plainly, Dick had lied to me. Also, subsequently, I asked Joan VanDrake (Probation Supervisor) what criteria she used to make in reference to how well I do pertaining to Number (3) above and possibly putting me on General Supervision or Regular Probation as opposed to Intensive Probation. In other words, Joan recommended the same as Dick above (i.e. meeting once per week with a telephone call). Joan said her response to this recommendation was, **"her education and experience."** Joan wouldn't even give me a 2 minute explanation of her criteria or example(s) of criteria used to making her decision or even two minutes of her time for that matter. In Joan's own words, **"I have done nothing wrong and have only done positive things"**. To me, this type of rationale would get Joan fired. I told Dick and Joan, concerning the nine months that has elapsed, the following benefits, for argument sorts, to get me off of Intensive Probation:

1 To date, I've met **all conditions of Probation**.

2   I have continually seen my Psychiatrist and Therapist and have continued on my medication regime.

3   I go to a Psycho – Social Club every Thursday morning (i.e. New Directions) and sometimes on Fridays.

4   At the Social Club I have access to a gym, weight room, and pool. This should help me physically and mentally.

5   I have weekly contact with members of my family, Mom & Step-Dad, Sisters, Brothers, Cousin, Grandmother, and Others.

6   I am pursuing another degree in Computer Science.

7   I go to church every week and on special/social occasions.

TO: Honorable Judge Manley letter dated February 01, 2000 (i.e., included was my travel concerns and more importantly, at this point, down grading Intensive Probation to General Supervision). Per Dick Press, I am still on Intensive Probation and am not allowed to visits outside the county. Also, recently, Judge Manley rejected my plea to see my Dad who lives outside the county (no reasons given). In this letter, I ask Judge Manley for me to be taken off the Intensive Probation Status to General Supervision, and per John E. E.'s (Assistant Public defender) recommendation, I should ask the Judge to be added to the Court's calendar and be appointed representation to argue and be taken off Intensive Probation. At this point I've been on Intensive Probation for a year; as noted, I could have been off Intensive Probation after 6 months, whereby, Joan VanDrake (Supervisor Probation) denied me this (no reason given). In other words, I've been on Intensive Probation twice the time I could have been off of it. In this letter also, I argue to Judge Manley my argumentative position(s) using the above (7) conditions that I've accomplished and met. Again, what more do I do to affirm my plea?

Per Honorable Judge T. Manley I sent him two more letters dated 3-03-00 and 3-20-00. As pointed out before and from above, I wanted myself to be present at a Court hearing in reference to the Judge putting me on the Court's Calendar to argue being taken off Intensive Probation to General Supervision. The Judge Manley never responded to all my letters; how unprofessional!

Per Honorable Manley, Mr. Daniel P. M., ESQ., and Mr. Ed N. respectively were written letters dated 12-11-00, 2-15-01, and 3-13-01 respectively. I know this issue diverts arguments concerning Intensive Probation reduced to General Supervision, but it's important; as such it concerns (1) Why was I discharged from the Criminal 4th degree burning of a bench in the town of Clarkson? (2) Why was I discharged from my Violation of Probation? (3) Why was I never afforded the Right TO A JURY TRIAL? And, (4) Why was I rever afforded the Right To have a Therapist/Psychiatrist testify on my behalf? Per Daniel P. M. on 4-05-01 at 5:30 PM Daniel said

Probation was not necessary and charge dismissed (satisfied as a result of Hearing). In other words, Daniel dodged me to confuse the issues; I'm still confused.

Judge Manley And Probation –

Travel Outside Of County /Country:

Per John E. E. (Assistant Public Defender) letters dated 12-29-99 (to John E. E.) & 1-14-00 (to Hon. Manley) made reference to an original letter dated 12-06-99 (to John E. E.). Letters dated 12-06-99 & subsequent 12-29-99 were copied and given to Judge Manley for a response. Among Intensive Probation concerns (as previously discussed), I wanted more importantly to discuss letting me travel as follows:

1   Travel outside of county – I wanted to see my father who lives in the Adirondack Region in ColdBrook, New York.
2   Travel to Israel- April 3 – 13, 2000 – I would travel with a group of Christians under Pastor/ Evangelist John Hagee. I needed answers to make my travel arrangements by 1-10-00. To argue my case to Judge Manley I used basically the same criteria as above per seven (7) criteria to Probation to get off Intensive probation to Regular Probation or General Supervision. My concern was what more do I have to do (or do you require of me) to argue my points for acceptance? In retrospect, you can tell Judge Manley that the Probation System has no systematic or set of criteria or goals to get off Probation. It's all subjective whereby all the Probation Officer or Supervisor needs to say is, **"my education and experience is all that's needed"**. It's not a fair system; not objective.

Per above letters to John E. E. (Assistant Public defender) dated 12-06-99 to 12-29-99, John wrote back a letter to myself dated 1-20-00. John said in his letter the following, "In reference to your letters regarding travel, as you are aware, I had spoken to Judge Manley in the past regarding the exact same request. **At that time it was denied.** I spoke again with Judge Manley about your request and he indicated it is between you and the Probation Department. Although I was the Attorney assigned to represent you on the underlying criminal charge, I do not continue to be your Attorney while you are on Probation. If you feel as though you are not being treated fairly by Probation, I suggest you write the Court explaining your position and request to be added to the Court's calendar. If Judge Manley feels as though you need representation, he can appoint you an Attorney if you cannot afford to hire one."

There seems to be a contradiction here. **First, John says Judge Manley mandated his denial my of request; and, later says it's between myself**

and Probation. Which is it, the Judge or Probation or a combination? Now on my Memo dated 1-25-00 (3:30 PM) I wrote about what I told Dick Press (Probation Officer) and Joan VanDrake (Probation Supervisor). They told me the wrong process in which to get permission to travel both outside the county and country as well. The process they told me was as follows:

1   The Probation Team would argue to the Judge why I should not be allowed to travel outside the county/country.
2   My Attorney would argue to the Judge why I should be allowed to travel outside the county/country.
3   The Judge would make a decision based on both arguments.

Per above referenced letter from John E. E. (Assistant Public defender) dated 1-20-00, John said Judge Manley told him my request to travel outside the county/country was between me and the Probation Department. There seems to be a big difference between Probation Officer's & Judge Manley's statement of policy as to processes concerning travel and other. Who's in charge here? Where's the communication? Per my Memo dated 2-15-00 (3:30PM), I met with Dick Press (Probation Officer) – concerning Israel trip decision. As you recall earlier in John E. E.'s letter dated 1-20-00 verbatim John says the Judge said it's between me and the Probation Department. In this Memo Dick Press, John E.E., and Judge Manley met in Court on 2-10-00 to discuss me going to Israel. My letter to John E. E. said I needed an answer by 1-10-00 and my letter to Judge Manley said I needed an answer by 1-25-00. I had to make an Israel trip final payment by 2-03-00. The point here; they met on 2-10-00 which is past my final payment deadline to go to Israel. Why hold a meeting between the three of them if I can't go anyway (i.e. their meeting is over due)? Stupidity! A final note, they should have contacted my Therapist for her input. Again, per John's letter dated 1-20-00 said any decision to travel was that of Probation and myself.

By Mark C. Russell

AN AFTER THOUGHT:

The Honorable Manley and Joan VanDrake (Probation Supervisor) both respectively approved me traveling outside the county on 6-21-99 and 8-06-99. Why so much negativity subsequent; these trips proved to be viable; not negative! The trips were approved as follows:

Honorable Manley (Monroe County Court Judge)
- Travel Order dated June 21, 1999
- Trip to Darien Lake July 25 – 27, 1999
- And one week in August to visit his dad in ColdBrook, New York

Joan VanDrake (Probation Supervisor) Travel Permit dated 8-06-99
- Attend Renaissance Faire in Sterling , New York
- Probationer will leave Monroe County, NY 8-07-99
- Travel with New Directions Club & Staff

Honorable Judge Moot:
Foreword:

The following is a history of my criminal activity:

Reference Taken From
Monroe County Office Of Probation – Community Corrections
Pre – Sentence / Social Investigation

LEGAL HISTORY

DATE	CHARGE	COURT	DISPOSITION
9/13/90	Criminal Mischief 3rd	Greece Town	11/5/90 PG to Att. Crim. Misch 4th, sent to Unconditional Discharge
12/08/90	Arson 3rd	Monroe County	9/24/92 PG to Criminal Mischief 4th 11/24/92 Sent to 3 years Prob. 11/28/94 Discharged

DATE	CHARGE	COURT	DISPOSITION
10/16/98	Arson 3rd	Monroe County	½/99 PG to Crim. Michief 3rd, sent. 5 yrs Prob. 5/4/00 VOP 11/2/00 discharged
4/27/00	Criminal Mischief 3rd	Clarkson Town	sat. by VOP 5/4/00
Last Offense	Criminal Mischief 3rd	Ogden Town	7/11/02 Conv Crim. Mischief 4th PSI pend. For 9/17/02

Per above, my last offense dated 7-09-01 was under the auspices of Judge Moot (Ogden Town Court). On the first four offenses I had pleaded guilty to a lessor charge and nobody heard about my history/ run-ins with the Federal Government (i.e. Government improprieties & illegalities). After my fifth criminal offense I had a Trial by Jury; FINALLY! I was sentenced on 9-17-02. The trial was narrowly tailored/scoped (between the Judge, Prosecutor, and Public Defender) whereby some, not all (complete), Government improprieties/ illegalities were exposed! My book gives an overall/more complete picture as to my position; and tells the truth of how our Government improprieties run. To me, the Government is a cesspool; Satan is working overtime.

Enhanced Diversion/Electronic Monitoring:
Per Judge Moot, I believe, that overall before and after sentencing he was too harsh and hard nosed when dealing with me. Judge Moot started by putting me on Enhanced Diversion/Electronic Monitoring Home Confinement Program Consent from 7-13-01 to 10-14-03. Initially I was under Supervision of a Mr. Florentino F.. I was told that that period of time (i.e. 7-13-01 to 10-14-03) was long; included was wearing an ankle bracelet monitoring me at all times and I was restricted to travel and confined to my condo. Per Judge Moot I was released to Enhanced Diversion – Electronic Monitoring on July 13, 2001. I was put under the auspices of Pre – Trial Services Corporation of The Monroe County Bar Association. I will say upfront, Judge Moot had it in for me. My records show (of which they may not be totally complete) four different Letters of Recommendation in which Pre – Trial Services Corporation Representatives Roxanne S. (CS/ED Case Manager/Team Leader) and Ms. Barbara R. (Post Release

Services Coordinator) wrote Judge Moot specific recommendation letters. These letters to Judge Moot each stated basically the same thing as follows: "Due to his continued compliance since July 13, 2001, this writer respectfully requests the Court consider downgrading Mr. Russell's release status from Enhanced Diversion – Electronic Monitoring to Contact Supervision." My records show four letters of this sort dated (there may be more that I don't know about) 2-15-02, 3-18-02, 4-01-02, and 4-23-02. Judge Moot, I believe, was too harsh and over zealous by denying accepting the Recommendations of these Pre-Trial Services Representatives. I believe that Pre – Trial Services Corporation Representatives Roxanne S. and Ms. Barbara R. have better insight as to my possible release status than does Judge Moot; these Representatives have had constant monitoring of me and constant supervision – as opposed to not so with Judge Moot. Again, Judge Moot is being too hard nosed. Satan, in guise!

Per Judge Moot's Review And Purview:
Reference Taken From
MONROE COUNTY OFFICE OF PROBATION – COMMUNITY CORRECTIONS
PRE-SENTENCE / SOCIAL INVESTIGATION
APPROVED BY:
Robert H. Probation Supervisor & Patricia E. D. Probation Officer

Per interview with Probation Department on 8-19-02 I gave some background information and discussed the present offense. This investigative report included statements from the Probation Officer as follows:

Per Defendant's Statement; "The defendant admitted guilt in the present offense but did not show remorse". I never indicated either way 'showing or not showing'. She's just trying to discredit me. Also, per Investigative Report, under the heading MENTAL HEALTH / AGENCY INVOLVEMENT – The Probation Officer wrote: "He stated that in 1989 he was dismissed from his job after handing out pamphlets that he authored entitled "Government Prosecution". It's not Prosecution, it's "Persecution".

Per Investigative Report Evaluative Analysis:
Defendant's Strengths
> College Education
> Sound Physical Health
Defendant's Problem Areas
> Mental Health Problems

Unemployment due to disablement from M.H. problems
History of similar offenses
Lack of responsibility for his criminal involvement
Lack of remorse

The Probation Officer says, "The defendant presents as mentally unstable individual who had trouble staying focussed for the interview... Given the defendant's criminal history and current mental health problems, incarceration appears warranted...based upon the aforementioned strengths and problem areas, it is felt the defendant's prognosis for lawful behavior is poor." RECOMMENDATION: INCARCERATION. As for, "prognosis for lawful behavior is poor", I state the following: My present offense was dated 7-09-01 and it's 4 years and 3 months later; plainly, I've stayed lawful. As for incarceration, I believe this Probation Officer and the Judge are too harsh and over zealous in both their judgements; they are just serving in the interest of the Federal Government. Satanic at best.

Per Judge Moot (Recommendation Letters):

I had six letters of recommendation (in my favor) prior to sentencing all of which stated/recommended for me to be put on Probation with "No Jail Time". These letters were dated from 9-05-02 to 9-17-02; and, included was Myself, my Dad, my Pastor, my Mom & Step-Dad, my Half-Sister, and my Sister. Also noted, my Psychiatrist (Chris) and Assistant Public Defender (Kevin K.) recommended "No Jail Time". Where is Judge Moot in the midst of all of this; what is he thinking? Flash-forward, the Judge had me "Serve Jail Time".

Per recommendation letter, I thought I would write a clip from my Pastor's letter, as follows: "I have served as Mark Russell's Pastor during the past five years. In previous years, Mark has served in positions of responsibility in the congregation: Financial Secretary, Elder, Evangelism, Usher, and Lector. He continued to attend worship faithfully in recent years but has been unable to serve in such positions due to his medical condition... but I hope that with help, he will be able to find a positive place in society." In addition, to the above letter, per Reverend Charles E. Alspaugh, I served as a Financial Counter and attended Bible Study Classes, and have served as Crucifer.

Per Judge Moot – Sentencing (9-17-02):

Per Criminal Mischief 4th, Judge Moot put me on three (3) years Probation and eight (8) weekends at the Monroe Correctional Facility, 750 East Henrietta Road, Rochester, New York from 2-21-03 to 4-12-03. Don't forget Enhanced Diversion/Electronic Monitoring. I believe the Judge should have never had me serve jail time. He was too harsh and over zealous. Again, Satan in guise.

Per Judge Moot – Midterm Probation Review:

I wrote Judge Moot a letter dated 1-19-04 to ask if I can get an Early Discharge from Probation which would be a Mid-Term Review (i.e. 11/2 years of the total three year probation term). Half term would expire as of 4-15-04. The Judge never wrote me back or responded to my letter; how unprofessional! In my letter, it depicts some of the more important Order And Conditions of Probation And My 100% Compliance as follows:

1   To Coach SUNY Brockport College Swim/Dive Team from 10-15-02 to 2-15-03. I in fact did complete this Term). Presently, I am doing voluntary computer work for my church and come Spring I hope to mow the church lawn.
2   Spend 8 weekends in the Monroe County Correctional Facility from 2-21-03 to 4-12-03.
3   Home Confinement to terminate on 10-14-03 (over two years on Home Confinement). Obey curfew hours monitored by an ankle bracelet.
4   Probation to start 10-15-02 and terminate 10-15-03 (Early Discharge of Probation).
5   To pay, in full, Restitution, Attorney fees (Mr. Kevin K.) and continue to pay $30.00/Month for an Administrative Fee.
6   Participate in a Mental Health Treatment Program.

The following depicts the 100% compliance in the numbers as outlined above:

1   Enclosed is a letter of Recommendation (See Appendix) from Dr. Gregory A. K. (SUNY Brockport College Head Swimming & Diving Coach). **I think it speaks for itself.** Also, as stated above, I plan to do future work for the church and college.
2   I had a 100% compliance for the 8 weekends served in the Correctional Facility.
3   I had 100% compliance in Home Confinement which included curfew, noted travel restrictions, and ankle bracelet. I am now off Home Confinement and ankle bracelet as of 10-14-03.
4   I was 100% for **ALL** conditional aspects included in the Orders And Conditions of Probation; Early Discharge was also written as a Condition and, should be BINDING if I was 100% compliant. Apparently, Judge Moot thought differently (No Early Discharge); Why?

5   I paid my Restitution 100% as well as 100% Attorney Fees and con-
     tinue to pay monthly Administrative Fees.

6   I 100% continually seek psychiatric care and take meds. Also, for
     your information, Mr. Doug C. (Probation Officer) and his Boss, sup-
     ported a decision to a Mid – Term 11/2 years Early Discharge. My
     Psychiatrist, Dr. Chris, also supports an Early Discharge of Probation.
     Plainly, the Honorable Judge Moot refused any kind of Early Discharge
     from Probation even though I was 100% totally compliant in the or-
     ders and conditions and the program itself. The Judge never gave any
     reasons to his siding to anybody including Myself, My Psychiatrist
     and Probation; Why?

Mr. Doug C. (Probation Officer) Memo dated 12-04-03
@ 11:00 AM – A final note per this meeting:
Mr. Doug C. said when he usually files for Early Probation Discharge the
Judge agrees. Well, if I was 100% compliant why did the Judge (Moot)
turn down my Early Discharge? Doug said I could have done nothing
more to get off Early Probation Discharge. Doug does not know why the
Judge was negative. Doug said he would see whether the Judge would
consider me getting off Probation after 11/2 years (Mid-Term Review).
Mr. Doug C. said there's no use of getting a Public Defender involved because the Judge had all the facts per Mr. Doug C.. * All and all, and all said
and done, The Honorable Judge Moot never did give me Early Discharge!
How Honorable!

CHAPTER 12

Miscellaneous Other
The Great Satan

By Mark C. Russell

TYPICAL INDIVIDUAL IN SATAN'S SYSTEM (AN EXAMPLE):

One of millions; look at recent news Congressman Patrick Kennedy (a good example) whereby, over the years, he was forced into Satan's System. Recently, he was caught in a driving violation under the influence and symptoms of Satan's System. Typical symptoms include depression, psychiatric counseling, and taking medication Ambien (for sleeping) and medication for anti Nausea. Patrick is just another statistic/individual sucked into Satan's System. Look at his family and relatives and their hardships; again, Satan's System.

Work Performance Appraisals (1986 – 1989):
I had several Work Performance Appraisals during this period of work and all were valued as, "Fully Successful". I also completed several work-related courses with no problem. See Appendix for Appraisals.

Government Oppression And Aggression:
The Government is trying very hard to get me to go back to work for them. They are harassing me vehemently and against the law. An example, during the 2002 – 2003 SUNY Brockport College Springboard Diving school year, a lady came to one of my Diving Practices, out of nowhere, and said she was from Maryland. Before she left, she asked me to visit Maryland. Someone (Government) paid this lady to try and get me back in Maryland where I once worked. I hate the Government for their oppression! I don't want to work for them again!

During the 2002 – 2003 SUNY Brockport College Springboard Diving School Year, someone put a Denver, Colorado hat (cap) at the Diving end of pool specifically so that I would not miss this cap (Denver, CO has a Government facility there). My point, tell the Government to leave me alone and respect my privacy!

On October 8, 2003 at 3:45 PM I found a note on my front door of my condominium which stated, ' Sorry I missed you' and it was signed by a Mr. Sam with a phone number on the note. I got so upset that I threw the note away. A Mr. Sam worked as a Senior Auditor and a coworker at the above mentioned DCAA – Field Detachment in Annapolis, Maryland (Westinghouse-Oceanic Division). As inferred, I do not want a Mr. Sam or any Government Associate to have any contact with me whatsoever, especially a former coworker. **Jim, to me, was Trespassing and Harassing me; Stay off my property!**

The System:
- Whenever a newsperson, sportsperson, or other, says that **"the devil is in the details"**; believe me this can be taken literally and figuratively and shouldn't be taken lightly.
- In the Satanic System I've been describing, part of the system tries you to get a tattoo(s). If you see somebody that has tattoo(s) most likely they circummed to the System.
- Under this same Satanistic System, the system tries to get you to get some sort of body piercing. If you see somebody with body piercing most likely they circummed to Satan's System.
- At one point in time, I've had relatives tell me that I could be killed trying to expose the Government (The Great Satan of America) and its system.

Girlfriends/Boyfriends and Wives/Husbands:
As part of Satan's System, Satan and or his entourage will try to hook you up with someone within the System to someone who is not in the System. The ultimate goal of Satan is to get anyone and everyone hooked into his System as well; by any means.

Grandmother Having Angina Attacks (1986-87):
My Dad and Grandmother came to Baltimore, Maryland to visit me at my condo. During this period in time my Grandmother was having some Angina attacks. Surprisingly enough I was having, at this time as well, some mild Angina attacks myself (even so I did nothing about it). Never before or after had I had these mild attacks. I believe the Government had their dirty hands in this mess.

Placebo Psychiatric Medications and Constipation Medicines:
Ever since 1987 to date I've taken many different psychiatric medications. Only one had any effect on me; Haldol. Haldol was so powerful and de-bilitating they took me off of it. I also originally took Chlorpromazine and it only took effect on me for two nights; no effect thereafter. I believe that I have played the part of a **guinea pig**; subject to the Government's mon-itoring and watching. All other medications that **I have taken have had no effect at all**; my Psychiatrist, in essence, says that's good. I responded to my psychiatrist that I wanted to, at times, feel some sort of relief by taking these meds of which I felt nothing and where the psychiatrist said that's good. I only came to the conclusion that I was taking placebos instigated by the Government, and again, I am a guinea pig. Again, I **feel nothing**; no relief. The psychiatrist then had nothing to say.

Sometime during the early 1990's I was in the Rochester, NY Psychiatric Center (RPC). For the first time in my life, ever, I had constipation. A doctor gave me a bottle of a lime substance and said if I drink the whole bottle that I would for sure have a bowel movement. In effect, I did not have a bowel movement even after taking this whole bottle of a lime substance. However, I did have a bowel movement only several days later subsequent to taking the bottle of a lime substance; I had to go to extremes. Again, I'm only a guinea pig instigated by the Government or Satan's System subject to their monitoring.

Status Quo: Today, I still have to go to extremes to have a bowel movement. Currently, my specialized doctor (of GASROENTEROLOGY & HEPATOLOGY) tells me I have Chronic Ideopathic Constipation (e.g. unknown cause of constipation). This is typical of the Satanic System I'm describing throughout my book. My doctor tells me I'm young to have such a disease. As such, the Government is trying any means to get me back into their Satanic System and back to work for them again (i.e. as their puppeteer of course).

Prostitution:
If someone in Satan's system (i.e. the Government) wants bad enough prostitution or likewise this person can get it; take my word for it.

Some recent System Notables:
5/16/08: Directly crossing my path on route 31 in my hometown, Brockport, was a van with **National Security** written on it. This is illegal surveillance, ect., on me which is a **felony**.

10/03/08: Directly in front of me near routes 19 & 31 in my hometown, Brockport, was a car with a hat in the back window that had written on it **"Security"**. Again, illegal surveillance, ect., on me.

5/20/08: I had just got done with mowing the church lawn (in Spencerport) with almost nobody around as usual in the parking lot. I came across a car in this lot with **"Bay"** written on the license plate. The Bay is where I used to work for the Government. In other words the Government wants me back to work at the Bay. Again, illegal surveillance, ect., on me.

8/01/08: I had just got done with mowing the church lawn (in Spencerport) with almost nobody around as usual in the parking lot. I came across a car in this lot with **"Maryland"** written on the license plate. As you know Maryland is where I used to work for the Government. In other words the

Government wants me back to work there again. Again, illegal surveillance, ect., on me.

6/17/08 & 8/11/08: On both these dates at my Doctor's office I was parked right outside the Doctor's office in the parking lot with a car with **"Bay"** written on its license plate. This is the same situation per above on date 5/20/08 (refer to above date: 5/20/08). Again, illegal surveillance, ect., on me.

11/02/08: I was on my way to my parent's home , as usual every Sunday, and stopped at the A-Plus store for my newspaper. A person pulled next to me with an **FBI sweat shirt**. Need I say more. Again, illegal surveillance, ect., on me.

11/11/08: I was traveling on Route 490 East to my Doctor's appointment and a car passed me with a license plate that said, **Special Agent**. Bells are ringing again. Again, illegal surveillance, ect., on me.

Churches I gave out classified information to:

1   Trinity Lutheran Church – (9-02-90 @ 9:30 AM) – After the sermon I approached the Pastor and asked him if I could make a short announcement. He did not say either way so I started to give the announcement. I gave the announcement in a calm, diplomatic, collective, and professional manner. I even wore my best suit after having it dry-cleaned and pressed. My speech was made in front of the pulpit until my Step-Dad started making his move up the aisle so I stepped (as facing the congregation) to the far right of the church and up about a 3rc of the way. My speech was as follows: Folks I would like to give you a short announcement. I want to do this as diplomatically as possible. The FBI indirectly informs me that they need competent evidential matter as to what I'm about to say. So listen carefully please. The U.S. have submarines off the East Coast of Russia in the Sea of Okhotsk or Sea of O. for short. These submarines are looking at Russian Rocket Wreckage. These submarines are the world's deepest going submarines whereby no other submarine has ever achieved these submerged depths before. The U.S. makes these submarines at Westinghouse (Oceanic Division), Annapolis, Maryland next to the Chesapeake Bay Bridge. This is plainly Top Secret Information and I worked in a Top Secret environment. The Government persecutes their employees by having their right to privacy invaded, they harass their employees, and they trespass. You are people of God

and should take interest. So I will be available after church. Again, the FBI will be coming around and you are witnesses as to what I said." During the announcement my Step-Dad notoriously walked toward the altar and stood between the pulpit and lectern. In his hypocrite way he told the congregation to pray for me and disregard what I had said. I told the Congregation to disregard what he says. Then I left the Nave to set up my pamphlets & leaflets at the back door of the church. My Step-Dad stayed at the front of the Congregation and most likely delivered some untrue statements concerning myself without my hearing.

2   St. Elizabeth Anne Seton Church (Hamlin 9-09-90 @ 8:30 AM) – I had went to the 8:30 AM Mass at this church whereby the Church had a good amount of people attending. I told the Reverend classified information and several other people. I asked the Reverend if I could introduce myself before the Congregation and he said no. He thought it would start a precedent. I asked him if this was like when Jesus (before the pharisees) could not heal on Sunday? He said yes.

3   Trinity Emmanuel Lutheran Church 9-09-90 @ 11:00 AM) – I went to the 11:00 AM service whereby the seats were pretty much filled. I told the Reverend classified information and several other people (as they were leaving the Nave). I would tell each family as they walked out. As I was leaving I said to the Pastor don't forget about the U.S. Submarines in Russia. He said he wouldn't.

Police Harassment 8-25-90 @ 2:00 PM:

Approximately 2:00 PM I was going door to door on the east side of Banks Road near Caledonia when I was stopped by Caledonia Police; he said that he was doing an investigation because someone called in and complained about my material (e.g. pamphlets & leaflets). He said I was required by law to give him identification. I handed him my license. He required me to sit in the back of his car to wait for the Sheriff's Sergeant Livingston County, NY (it was this Sheriff's jurisdiction); not his. I had requested to stand outside of his car but he said no. Some lady at a house next to the house I was parked at came over and discussed something with the Caledonia Policeman but I could not hear their discussion. I was in the back seat of his car. In my travels that day I did not see the residents either at the house I was parked or next door with the lady who talked with the Caledonia Police. The reason being that I had just pulled into the driveway of where I was parked when the Caledonia Policeman called me over. Then the Sheriff's Sergeant- Livingston County arrived after a long wait and talked with the Caledonia Policeman while I was still in the Caledonia's Police car. The same lady next door came over again and talked with the Sheriff's Sergeant while I was still in Caledonia's Policeman's car. Both Policemen exchanged my license. After awhile both Police came over to let me out of the police car (I was locked in his car for at least half an hour and I really feel this is a violation of my rights because I was doing nothing wrong). I got out of the car and he started asking me personal questions. I asked him if I was under arrest and he said no – not yet. Then I said am I required by law to answer his questions? He said yes. He said if I did not he would take me to his Livingston County Office. I said OK. I told him where my former address was at 9 Pine Hill Road Spencerport, NY 14559. I told him I was not living at this address any more but I was living somewhere else. I told him that 9 Pine Hill Road was my parents' address and gave him their phone number. I offered my mailing address but he would not take this information even after he had told me the reason he wanted this information was to get in touch with me later if he needed to. How is he going to get in touch at 9 Pine Hill Rd. if I don't live there anymore? He asked me what Department of the Government I used to work for and I said Department of Defense. He then asked me some more questions about work and I told him that it was classified but he could get in touch with the FBI if he wanted to. The Sergeant said that I was required by Law to give him a copy of my pamphlet and leaflet. I gave him a copy of my pamphlet and he already had a copy of my leaflet. He said I was not on any wanted list and I told him I never have been arrested nor have I ever done anything against the Law except give away classified information. I asked him twice if he was going to contact the FBI about this information and his reply was that a report would be written up and filed and would be on file if the FBI wanted to look at it. He never said that he was going to contact the FBI. The Caledonia Policeman told me I may be required to get a permit to do what I was doing. The Sheriff asked me if I was asking for contributions. I said no. Then I said I was just handing out these pamphlets and I was not soliciting. He said he did not know whether I needed a permit or not and told me to go to the Caledonia Town Hall. He told me not to hand out any more pamphlets and/or leaflets until I ask about the permit and said if I did hand out any he would arrest me for disorderly conduct (of which I'm not guilty). He himself said that the people who called in said that I looked like a suspicious character because there have been several robberies in the area, not that I had disorderly conduct. I asked him if I could leave and he said yes. A final note; I told the Sergeant that I've been to the Town Halls of Greece, Gates, Webster, Penfield, and the City of Rochester and none of these areas required a permit to hand out pamphlets & leaflets. I believe I could sue him for restraining my Constitutional Rights especially since he did not know whether I needed a permit or not.

Final Highlight: 2006 - present Illegal
Government Surveillance Statistics:

The following are statistics for the calendar years 2006 to present that the Government has been tracking and surveillancing me. These statistics in and of themselves won't particularly evidence illegal surveillance, etc., but, these statistics, put together, is more than enough to tell me, or other, that the Government is illegally surveillancing and harassing me. I believe this to be illegal in nature and I believe the Government has been doing this type of illegal surveillancing on me since my first date of employment (Jan. of 1986). The Government follows me everywhere unscrupulously. I rarely leave the house and when I do I waste no time whether it be grocery, post office, gas station, doctor's office, family, etc.. Again, the Government just won't leave me alone; they are illegally following, surveillancing, tracking, trespassing, and harassing me in and out of my home (i.e. everywhere). Since the Government wants me back to work for them (i.e. for security reasons) they are in effect indirectly telling me six places I can go back to work for them: Baltimore, MD; Charlotte, N.C.; Dallas, Texas; Myrtle Beach, S.C.; Denver, CO; and Boston, Massachusettes. While I was working for the Government these six places were of interest because we did business with these six places. By working for the Government, this which, in effect, will keep me in the physical realm and the property of "The Navy" and helps preserve the sensitivity of the Top Secret information of the Navy by living and breathing this environment. Technically and forthright speaking this is still very much illegal; that's why the Government's indirect approach of trying not to leave an audit trail.

The following are the 2006 Illegal Government Surveillance Statistics:

1   **OLD NAVY** (T-Shirts, TV, etc.): The following are dates and places where people **have directly crossed my paths** wearing "Old Navy" attire. Since my previous employment was with the Government and with auditing Top Secret Navy Contracts, the Government wants me back to work for them (i.e. for security reasons). My Government job dealt with "The Navy" and Top Secret Navy contracts; therefore, can you see this indirect connection of "Old Navy" attire and working for the Navy again. Again, wherever I go, which is not too far or often, people specifically and purposely cross my path wearing "Old Navy" attire; I believe this is propagated by the Government. This, in effect, is telling me to go back to work for the Government. The following represent people (dates and places) specifically directed to come directly into my path: 1-18: Walmart BKPT.; 1-27: Cathy's TV Navy Program; 2-14: Navy Pict. Weg. Photo; 2-23: Navy Cap @ Dentist;

3-04: Wegman's Bkpt.; 3-20: Home Depot; 4-06: Navy Cap Home Depot; 4-08: Wegman's Bkpt.; 4-12: Main St. Bkpt.; 4-26: 2X Navy car Main St. Bkpt.; 4-29: 2X Bkpt. High School; 4-30: Sppt.; 5-06:Clarkson Auto 11:00AM;5-08: Wegman's Bkpt.; 5-15: Aldis & Army T-shirt; 5-22: SUNY Bkpt. Pool; 5-27: 2X Walmart Greece; 6-04: Home Depot And Gas; 6-11: Home Depot And Walmart Bkpt.; 6-28: Car Rt. 19 Bkpt.;6-30: Aldis and Army T- Shirt; 7-02: Aldis and Dicks Sporting Goods; 7-08: 2X Wegmans Brockport; 7-21: Bank Brockport; 8-11: U.S. Navy Cap @ Zac's Graduation; 8-23: Walmart @ Brockport; 8-25: Circuit City; 9-03: Kwik Fill @ Spencerport; 9-17: Aldis Brockport; 10-01: Dollar Store @ Brockport; 10-15: Hess @ Brockport; 10-17: Wegmans Greece; 10-29: Aldis @ Brockport;   11-05: Aldis @ Brockport; 11-27: AAA Coat saying "U.S. Navy"; 12-20: Radiology @ Brockport Hospital; 12-26: Greece Mall.

2 **Charlotte, North Carolina** (TV ADS, T-Shirts, etc.): As previously noted, while working for the Government we did business with Charlotte, North Carolina. Indirectly, the Government is, in effect, telling me that I can go back to work for the Government in Charlotte, North Carolina for near future employment. Here you are able to see that by N. C. T-shirts being directed in my path at various places around Rochester, New York saying "North Carolina", this is what the Government wants me to see and react in this indirect way (i.e. pick one of six places to go back to work for the Government). Also, included under this category are TV advertisements concerning Charlotte, North Carolina (i.e. gourmet coffee, furniture ads, etc.). I, in effect, have documented some of these TV advertisements. Another inclusion is that of AAA (Auto Insurance @ place of business in Greece, New York) whereby on two occasions two independent people talked about North Carolina and got maps to North Carolina right next to me while I was at the AAA site at the front counter and at an office desk. What are the chances that of my only two visits to AAA, and at that particular time and place, there was someone both times, getting North Carolina inquiries. Finally, this category includes some other miscellaneous items as designated. The following are dates and places where people **have directly crossed my paths** wearing "North Carolina" attire, TV advertisements (i.e. channels & times) concerning Charlotte, North Carolina, AAA (Auto club) concerning North Carolina, and other miscellaneous: 1-27: TV Advertisement Channel 13, 5:30 PM Charlotte Furniture; 2-14: North Carolina Patch @ Dollar Store Brockport; 2-17: TV Advertisement Channel 13, 2:15 & 7:00PM Charlotte Furniture Advertisement; 2-18: Channel 8, 2:05 PM Charlotte Carolina Commercial; 3-03: Channel 13, 6:10 PM Charlotte,

North Carolina Furniture Advertisement; 3-09: Channel 35, 8:00 PM Charlotte Gourmet Coffee Advertisement; 3-28: Channel 64, 8:15 PM Charlotte Gourmet Coffee Advertisement; 4-05: Channel 20, 7:38 PM Charlotte, North Carolina Commercial; 4-18: AAA Man next to me talked about North Carolina; 4-28: Channel 20, 8:15 PM Charlotte, North Carolina Commercial; 5-02: AAA Man @ Map department Talked about North Carolina; 5-21: Channel 10, 9:25 PM Charlotte, Gourmet Coffee Advertisement; 6-12: SUNY Brockpport Pool; 7-04: Music on hold /phone to Loews played North Carolina song; 8-06: Channel 23, 8:30 PM North Carolina Advertisement and Denver advertisement; 8-25: Seymour Library In Brockport; 8-28: SUNY Brockport Divers/Coach Talked to me about North Carolina and Lisa Cole/ Coach Wore North Carolina T-Shirts my first week of Coaching; 11-17: Channel 48, 12:50 PM TV Advertisement About North Carolina Holiday; 12-19: License Plate Route 31 and Route 19 in Brockport; 12-25: A distant relative brought up North Carolina – about her relatives in North Carolina @ my sister's house on Christmas.

3   **Dallas, Texas** (T-Shirts): Here again, while working for the Government, we did business in Dallas, Texas. Again, the Government is indirectly telling me a place I can work for in the near future; Dallas Texas. By the same scenario with the Navy T-Shirts above this was done by flashing a T-Shirt in front of me with Dallas, Texas written on the T-Shirt at a store in Greece. I probably missed more of these statistics over time but did record one statistic as someone **crossing my direct path** at a store as follows: 2-01: 9:00 AM Loew's T-Shirt.

4   **Myrtle Beach, South Carolina** (T- Shirts): Here again, while working for the Government, we did business in Myrtle Beach, South Carolina. Again, the Government is telling me a place I can work for in the near future; Myrtle Beach, South Carolina. Some more people that crossed my direct path out and about around Rochester, New York is as follows: 2-03: Bart Peters (my plumber) wore a Myrtle Beach T- Shirt; 7-16: @ Home Depot someone **crossed my direct path** with a Myrtle Beach T-Shirt; 10-08: @ Wegmans Brockport someone crossed my direct path with a Myrtle Beach T-Shirt.

5   **Denver, Colorado** (T-Shirt, Vehicles, and TV): Here again, while working for the Government, we did business in Denver, Colorado. Again, the Government is telling me a place I can work for in the near future; Denver, Colorado. Some more people that crossed my direct path out and about around Rochester, New York is as follows: 1-10: @ Seymour Library in Brockport a person **crossed my path** with a T-Shirt; 3-23: A Truck with Colorado written on it in Spencerport crossed my path; 3-24: A Truck with Colorado written on it in Greece

crossed my path; 7-05: @ Seymour Library in Brockport a person crossed my path with a T-Shirt; 7-08: A Truck with Colorado written on it in Brockport Wegmans crossed my path; 8-06: Denver Colorado TV Advertisement on Channel 23 @ 8:30 PM; 11-27: @ Home Depot Greece person with Colorado T-Shirt crossed my path.

6   **Bay License Plate:** While working for the Government, we were located on the Chesapeake Bay Bridge in Maryland. I believe this showing of "Bay" license plates around Rochester, NY, directly in my paths on the road, are indicative of the Government wanting me to go back to work for them at this site or on the said Bay. As said before, this is one of six places the Government wants me to go back to work for them. As follows are places of interest where **I had crossed directly in my path** Bay License plates on vehicles: 1-14: Route 31 and Owens Road; 1-16: Route 31 and Route 531; 2-02: @ my CPA'S in Greece; 2-06: Main Street in Brockport; 2-21: Walmart in Brockport; 2-24: Route 104 in Greece; 3-06: Dental Associates 11:15 AM Greece; 3-15: Wegmans Brockport; 5-05: Main street Brockport; 5-07: Ogden Parma TLR; 6-16: South Avenue Brockport; 7-19: SUNY Brockport Campus; 8-17: Next to Trinity Lutheran Church; 8-29: Rite Aid Brockport; 9-26: SUNY Brockport Parking; 10-15: Wegmans Brockport; 10-18: Route 104 Rochester; 10-19: Route 104 Spencerport; 10-22: Dominos Pizza Brockport; 11-02: Office Max Greece; 11-08: Route 104 Marriott Greece.

7   **Maryland** (Various): As you know by now I worked for the Government in Maryland and the Government would love me to go back to work for them in Maryland. To me, the Government is harassing and trespassing my world by the following Maryland references during 2006: 1-19: While at an airline layover in Detroit @ gate B1 @ 11:20 AM a man talked and mentioned living in Delaware and drove to work each day to Baltimore – too much a coincidence to me; his conversation directed to me. At my workplace a secretary also traveled from Delaware to work. On this same gate/flight in seat A-D @ 12:05 PM flight 3524 a different man brought up Maryland – also too much of a coincidence in that this was **directed to me to be heard**; 1-22: At a Detroit Airline terminal a man was carrying a carry-on luggage which had written on it "NSA". To me this was the Government telling me that this man was associated with the "National Security Administration" spying on me – How deplorable! In my words – leave me alone! 5-05: On TV channel 63 @ 2:40 PM there was an Advertisement with destination Maryland on it (again, the Government wants me to go back to work for them); 5-13: On TV channel 63 @ 6:25 PM there was an advertisement that said Destination Maryland (again, Government

propagation); 11-27: AAA (Auto insurance place in Greece) again like Charlotte, North Carolina @ AAA above here we have a lady next to me talking about Maryland (to me this is not coincidental); 12-16: @ United Postal Service (UPS) in Brockport a lady talked about Baltimore, Maryland.

8   **Army** (T-Shirts): While working in Maryland we did some work pertaining to the Army of which I have no recollection anything of it. But, I believe this is another alternative in which the Government may want me back to work for them. Here are some dates and places that follows where Army T-Shirts were **paraded in front me** in direct line of my path: 4-12: I saw an Army T-Shirt with somebody wearing an Army T-Shirt in my back yard in Brockport; 7-02: I saw another Army T-Shirt @ Corners in Spencerport; 7-14: saw another Army T-Shirt at a gas station on Route 31 in Brockport; 7-30: I saw an Army Truck at Wegmans in Brockport; 8-11: I saw an Army T-Shirt @ my nephew's (ZAC) Graduation party.

9   **666 License Plates:** To cap this chapter off, we again take our hats off to a "Classified Look At The Great Satan of America: Top Secret Government Persecution". Here again, I believe The Great Satan is actively seeking me (and every Christian or Gentile) per 1 Peter 5:8 which says, " ... Your enemy the devil prowls around like a roaring lion for someone to devour." Satan is the Prince of this world (i.e. John 12:31) and per Revelation 13:16-18 dictates, "He forced everyone, small and great, rich and poor, free and slave, to receive a mark on his right hand or his forehead, so that no one could buy or sell unless he had the mark...His number is "666." Satan is designated and labeled by "666" and everyone in his System I'm describing, throughout this book, is forced to know this "666" as such and everyone in Satan's System keeps this "666" very highly secured and secretive throughout our world. I've also heard by word of mouth and by certain peoples, even certain addresses, forthcome "666", and finally by vehicle license plates crossing my direct paths around town had "666" written on them. Satan is actively seeking me and others and wants me and others to know and become a part of his System. The following are dates and places were vehicles had license plates with "666" written on them as they had **crossed my direct path:** 1-08: Trimmer Road Spencerport; 1-10: Owens Road and Route 104 & Greece; 1-30: Main Street Brockport; 1-31: Brockport Main Street and Route 31; 2-06: My sister's complex in Brockport; 2-07: Ho Ho Buffet Brockport; 2-27: Owens Road Brockport; 3-04: Wegmans Brockport; 3-19: Walworth, NY; 3-27: @ Dentist and Route 104 & Manitou Road; 5-12: K & K Food Mart Brockport; 5-14: Route 104 & Washington

Road; 6-26: South Avenue Brockport; 6-30: Aldis Brockport; 6-14: Dollar Store Brockport; 8-24: Movie Gallery & Owens Road; 10-17: Route 104 Greece; 12-13: @ Strand Theater Brockport.

The following are the 2007 to present Illegal Government Surveillance Statistics Categories. Since 2007 to present is much a repeat of 2006, for brevity purposes details are being left out and the same categories are specified repeating categories for the year 2006 as follows:

1 Old Navy (T-Shirts, TV, etc.)
2 Charlotte, North Carolina (T-Shirts, TV, etc.)
3 Dallas, Texas (T-Shirts)
4 Myrtle, Beach, South Carolina (T-Shirts)
5 Denver, Colorado T-Shirts, Vehicles, TV)
6 Bay License Plate
7 Maryland
8 Army (T-Shirts)
9 666 License Plates

***Update of recent contacts & dates relative to immedi-
ate above categories 1,2,6,7,9 for the year 2009:***

1) **Old Navy** (T-Shirts, TV, ect.): 1/23,2/08,2/19,4/13,4/17,5/01,5/03,5/22,5/29,6/20,6/27,7/03,9/04,9/25,10/02,10/08,10/19,11/04.

2) **Charlotte, North Carolina** *(T-Shirts,TV, ect.): 1/26,6/08,7/09, & 8/28.*

6) **Bay License Plates:** 1/13,2/13,4/14,4/20,6/27,7/03,7/13,9/18,9/25,10/01,10/16,11/16,12/01,12/14.

7) **Maryland (Various):** 1/30,4/12,4/18,4/19,6/03,10/24,10/29.

9) **666 License Plates:**1/12, 2/15,3/08,4/14,6/13,9/08,9/17.

FBI – I've come into contact with the so called FBI twice in 2009: **(1)** 6/27/09 an **FBI T-Shirt** @ Bed, Bath, & Beyond store and **(2)** 10/19/09 a "**FBI JESUS**" cap @ Wegmans Grocery store

You may ask, what is next on the Government's agenda? The Government is going to try to forcefully try anything/everything to get me into their Satanic System again and work as a Government puppeteer. As discussed earlier in my book in detail, they may try a number of forceful things that may include: sleeplessness, acid reflux, abdominal pain, diabetes, constipation, chronic skin irritation, car wreck and much more not included here (please refer to chapter 4 for more detail). They do such things in an indirect way to try and hide their so called System and ways.

Insight: The Government is just trying to feel me out to ultimately become part of their system (Satan's system) and become a slave as such. Let me try to give some final insight. The Government wants to try to force anything it can on me subject to my condescention. I have chronic idiopathic constipation, chronic skin irritation, some sleeplessness, sparce abdominal pain, once an uncontrollable bowel movement (messy), acid indigestion, and many culminating things I've described earlier in this book. I hope this book satisfies your curiosity as to my plight.

CONCLUSION:

The contents of my book is self-conclusive. The Government and other systems are flagrantly breaking the law; aggressive, oppressive, domineering, harry, offensive, invasive, attacking, and incursive. Our society is becoming more and more pervasive of lawlessness. The Antichrist of which many Evangelists talk about today (during End Times) is coming soon whereby the Rapture is soon and is next on the Prophetic Calendar followed by the seven year Tribulation Period. And, then followed by the 1,000 year Reign. It is my contention that God will bless you for reading this book!

The End

APPENDIX

- IG Findings – Inspector General Office Audit
- Department Of The Navy- FBI – NIS Investigation
- Inter-office Memorandum – Oral Admonishment, Security Violation
- Oral Admonishment Reply – Grievance Reply To Above Inter-office Memorandum
- Springboard Diving Resume – History Of Springboard Diving Accomplishments
- Business Professional Resume – History Of Professional Business Experience
- Performance Appraisals – Federal Government
- Recommendation Letters
    ParkRidge Hospital
    the Summit Federal Credit Union
    SUNY Brockport Diving Coach

By Mark C. Russell

IG "FINDINGS" REGARDING AUDIT OF THE FIELD DETACHMENT

- Insufficient incurred cost coverage (e.g., no MAARS tests).
- Insufficient number of defective pricing audits.
- No systems reviews.
- Staffing shortfalls.
- High staff turnover.
- Lack of quality control program.
- Proposal audit deficiencies:
    - No math accuracy tests.
    - Little testing of labor hours.
    - Little testing of material quantities.
    - Omitted consideration of historical costs.
    - Quantitative measurement techniques not used.
    - Manual schedules prepared where computers could have been used.
- Workpapers inadequate (e.g., no source, purpose, or scope).
- Audit programs not used for planning and often not documented regarding performance.
- Permanent files deficient.
- No documentation of supervision.

DEPARTMENT OF THE NAVY

HEADQUARTERS
NAVAL INVESTIGATIVE SERVICE COMMAND
WASHINGTON, D.C. 20388
25 July 1990

The Honorable Daniel Patrick M.
United States Senate
28 Church Street, Suite 203
The Guaranty Building
Buffalo, NY 14202

Dear Mr. M.,
The Navy Office of Legislative Affairs has asked me to respond to your letter of June 5, 1990 regarding a letter you received from Mr. Mark C. Russell of Spencerport, NY.

Mr. Russell was the subject of a joint FBI-NIS investigation concerning his disclosure of classified information to numerous United States persons. He obtained access to the information while employed as an auditor with the Defense Contract Audit Agency, and was medically retired from that agency in June 1989, due to psychological disability. Mr. Russell believed that the Government was spying on him and had implanted listening devices in his teeth. During the investigation, Mr. Russell admitted to knowingly and intentionally disclosing the classified information.

The U.S. Attorney in Rochester, NY, declined to prosecute on the grounds that due to Mr. Russell's psychosis, criminal intent could not be formed. The criminal investigation was closed on March 9, 1990. No adequate administrative or civil remedy was found that could compel Mr. Russell's silence.

Mr. Russell was informed of the U.S. Attorney's decision and that this agency was no longer pursuing the investigation. Since that time, Mr. Russell has written numerous ranking figures in Government, the military and the press seeking to be arrested. I feel that corresponding with Mr. Russell will only encourage him to continue his writing campaign and make further disclosures and so I have not written to him directly.

I trust that this satisfies your inquiry.
Sincerely,

W. L. S., Jr.
Rear Admiral, JAGG, USN
Commander NISC

Inter-Office Memorandum
DATE: 21 April 1987
To: Mr. Mark Russell
FROM: Steve, Branch Manager
SUBJECT: Oral Admonishment, Security Violation

This serves as an official record of our 10 April 1987 discussion of the 20 February 1987 series of events which resulted in the destruction certification of classified documents not actually destroyed. Although we are satisfied that no compromise of sensitive information occurred as a result of the subject procedural noncompliance, the incident is reportable as a security violation.

Although security is all of our responsibility, you must be constantly aware of your responsibilities, and if unsure about certain procedures or requirements, must inquire as to the propriety of any action, especially when you are a party to that action. We are confident that you will exercise such discretion in your continuing role as an auditor in the Field Detachment.

Steve
Branch Manager

DATE: 19 May 1987
TO: Steve, Branch Manager
FROM: Mark C. Russell
SUBJECT: Reply to Attached Oral Admonishment, Security Violation

This serves as an official record (reply) to our 10 April 1987 and 01 May 1987 discussion of the 20 February 1987 series of events which resulted in the destruction certification of classified documents not actually destroyed. In reference to your attached letter, Inter-Office Memorandum (Oral Admonishment, Security Violation) dated 21 April 1987, I believe that the said Oral Admonishment against myself should become void.

Although security is all of our responsibility, and that I must be constantly aware of my responsibilities even if unsure about certain procedures or requirements and inquire as to the propriety of any action when I am a party to such an action; I believe, in this case, that the primary and ultimate responsibility remains at the management/supervisory level. My reasons for this belief are as follows:

1   Even though I was one of the parties to the said security violation, I (being a GS-7 and a newcomer to the organization) had not received any supervision/training to the actual procedures or important implications of destroying documents. I was merely told to help with the destruction process and tried to do just that.
2   It has been pointed out in our 10 April 1987 discussion that the process and understanding of document destruction may or may not be clear-cut. If it is clear-cut, then why did a GS-12 (another party to the said action and has been aboard since January of 1983) receive the same Oral Admonishment? Could the reason be that there were no established procedures?
3   I, as a new comer, have not received any formal training on any security procedures.
4   Most important, there were no established procedures for the destruction of documents. Establishing such procedures would have provided ordinary care in the prevention of the said "procedural noncompliance". Whose responsibility is this?

I am confident that in the future such matters will be exercised with more discretion on my part but hope that preventative measures are established on the part of those responsible to deter such violations.

Mark C. Russell
Enclosure
Cc: Kenneth E. P.

MARK C. RUSSELL

OBJECTIVE
Seeking a challenging and rewarding position as Diving Coach.

EDUCATION
SUNY OSWEGO, *Syracuse, New York*
Education. 9/89 – 5/94 G.P.A. (3.25)
ROCHESTER INSTITUTE OF TECHNOLOGY, *Rochester, New York*
Degree: M.S. Accounting (November 1985) G.P.A. (3.13)
Major: Advanced Accounting
UNIVERSITY OF KENTUCKY, *Lexington, Kentucky*
Degree: B.S. Accounting 1983 G.P.A. (3.18)
Major: Accounting
Strong Financial Background

DIVING COACHING EXPERIENCE
SUNY Brockport
Head Diving Coach 2002 – 2003. Qualified diver top 10 in Conference.
General
Coached Spencerport, Brockport, and Churchville-Chili High Schools (various).
University of Rochester
Coached College diving 1983 - 1984. Qualified diver Division III Nationals.
MCC Marauders
Coached divers of all ages 1982 – 1983.

DIVING ACCOMPLISHMENTS
University of Kentucky

Full diving scholarship	1980 – 1983
All conference	1980 – 1983
NCAA pre-qualifier	1980 – 1983
Most valuable award	1982
110% award	1983
Co-captain of swim team	1983

MEN'S ALL TIME TOP 10 DIVING PERFORMANCES AS OF 2009:

1-METER (6 DIVES)	8th 318.00 pts. 1983
1-METER (11 DIVES)	4th 489.15 pts. 1983
3-METER (6 DIVES)	6th 353.25 pts. 1982
3-METER (11 DIVES)	4th 530.75 pts. 1983

Spencerport High School

All American	1976-77, 1977-78, 1978-79.
State Champion	1976-77, 1977-78, 1978-79.
All County	1976-77, 1977-78, 1978-79.
Undefeated	1976-77, 1977-78, 1978-79.
Letter Award	**1974- FIRST 8th GRADER IN NYS to ever receive award 1975-76, 1976-77, 1977-78, 1978-79**
Most Valuable	1977-1979.
Empire St. Games	*1978 (1st and 2nd places).*
	1979 (1st place).
	1981 (two 1st places).
	1982 (1st and 3rd places).

National Championship

Junior Olympics	1977 Qualified and participated

MARK C. RUSSELL

OBJECTIVE
Seeking a challenging and rewarding position as Diving Coach.

AUDITING
Audited pricing proposals and contract briefs, bid and proposal reviews, internal control reviews, forward pricing reviews and incurred costs. Prepared financial statements, analyzed and prepared balance sheets and income statements for compilation and review reports. Computer literate – generated financial reports using an IBM – PC. Conducted – capital asset inventory audits, wrote compliance/non-compliance resultant reports.

TAXES
Prepared individual, partnership and corporate tax returns. Utilized 1040 and FAST TAX for individual tax returns.

BOOKKEEPING
Posted to accounts receivable ledger and completed monthly billings, aging accounts, trial balances, petty cash, and bank deposits.

PAYROLL
Data entry and payroll reconciliation.

SHIPPING/RECEIVING
Inventory control, delivery of medical supplies.

EMPLOYMENT HISTORY
- The Health Association, Main Quest Treatment Center, Rochester, New York, Data Control Clerk, 8/96-9/96
- Summit FCU, Rochester, New York, Accounting Clerk Intern, 1/96-3/96
- Park Ridge Hospital, Rochester, New York Receiving Clerk, 5/95-12/95
- Landmark Industries, Rochester, New York, Payroll Clerk, 6/93-8/94
- Defense Contract Audit Agency, Annapolis, MD and Rochester, NY, Auditor, 1/86-2/89
- Goldstein & Viele, CPA, Rochester, NY, Accountant, 2/85-5/85
- Frederick J. Stoffel, CPA, Rochester, NY, Accountant, 10/83-5/84
- Eastman Kodak Co., Rochester, NY, Corporate Auditor (Summer Professional Program), 1982

- Modex Building Supplies, Rochester, NY, Bookkeeper (Summer Position), 1981

EDUCATION

- University of Kentucky, Lexington, Kentucky- B.S., Accounting, 1983 GPA (3.18)
- Rochester Institute of Technology, Rochester, NY-M.S., Accounting, 1985 GPA (3.13)
- State University of NY, Oswego, NY-Education- Various Courses, 1989-94 GPA (3.25)

By Mark C. Russell

PERFORMANCE APPRAISAL

DEFENSE CONTRACT AUDIT AGENCY
FIELD DETACHMENT AUDITOR
AS OF 30 MARCH 1987

TAKEN FROM OFFICIAL FORM (DCAA FORM 1317-5):

ADJECTIVE RATING RANGE:
OUTSTANDING, 270-300; SUPERIOR, 210-269; FULLY SATISFACTORY,
100-209; MINIMALLY SATISFACTORY, 50-99; UNSATISFACTORY, 0-49

Individual element rating levels are:
O = Outstanding (3 points)
FS = Fully Successful (1 point)
U = Unacceptable (0 points)
E = Exceeds Fully Successful (2 points)
M = Minimally Successful (.5 points)

APPRAISER'S COMMENTS:
Mr. Russell has performed at the fully satisfactory as a GS-7, Auditor
Trainee. He has met the performance criteria while serving his proba-
tionary initial year as a DCAA auditor, and therefore, I recommend his
promotion to GS-9.

Per performance appraisal I received a point total of "140 points".

Signed by

Mark C. Russell
Davide
Steve

PERFORMANCE APPRAISAL

DEFENSE CONTRACT AUDIT AGENCY
FIELD DETACHMENT AUDITOR
AS OF 13 MARCH 1988

TAKEN FROM OFFICIAL FORM (DCAA FORM 1409-1):

ADJECTIVE RATING RANGE:
OUTSTANDING, 270-300; SUPERIOR, 210-269; FULLY SATISFACTORY,
100-199; MINIMALLY SATISFACTORY, 50-99; UNSATISFACTORY, 0-49

Individual element rating levels are:
O = Outstanding (3 points)
FS = Fully Successful (1 point)
U = Unacceptable (0 points)
E = Exceeds Fully Successful (2 points)
M = Minimally Successful (.5 points)

APPRAISER'S COMMENTS:
Mark was on extended sick leave from 12 August 1987 through 3 October
1987.

Per performance appraisal I received a point total of "120 points".

Signed by

Mark C. Russell
Davide
Walter

By Mark C. Russell

PERFORMANCE APPRAISAL

DEFENSE CONTRACT AUDIT AGENCY
AS OF 13 MARCH 1988

TAKEN FROM OFFICIAL FORM (DCAA FORM 1409-1):

ADJECTIVE RATING RANGE:
OUTSTANDING, 270-300; SUPERIOR, 210-269; FULLY SATISFACTORY, 100-199; MINIMALLY SATISFACTORY, 50-99; UNSATISFACTORY, 0-49

Individual element rating levels are:
O = Outstanding (3 points)
FS = Fully Successful (1 point)
U = Unacceptable (0 points)
E = Exceeds Fully Successful (2 points)
M = Minimally Successful (.5 points)

APPRAISER'S COMMENTS:
None.

Per performance appraisal I received a point total of "106 points".

Signed by

Mark C. Russell
Tammy
Ben

PARK RIDGE HOSPITAL

Rochester, New York 14626
Reference

To whom it may concern:

This letter will serve as a reference for Mark C. Russell of 9 Pine Hill Road, Spencerport, NY 14559. Mark Russell was placed at Park Ridge Hospital through Work Guide. During his time with us (5/95 – 11/95) Mark demonstrated the following attributes:

- Punctual
- No excessive absenteeism
- advanced notification of requested time off
- worked well with others
- worked well independently
- able to work with minimal amount of supervision
- asked questions to clarify duties and/or instructions
- ability to adapt when department was short staffed
- seeked out additional tasks
- showed initiative to learn new functions
- personal grooming habits met the established guidelines

All in all, Mark was a benefit to us during his tenure here.

Sincerely,
Timothy F. Z.
Inventory Coordinator

THE SUMMIT FEDERAL CREDIT UNION

Canal Ponds Business Park
100 Marina Drive
Rochester, New York 14626
Telephone (585) 453-7000

March 29, 1996

To whom it may concern:

Mark Russell worked at The Summit Federal Credit Union as a temporary assistant in the accounting department. He joined The Summit on Wednesday, January 3, 1996 and worked approximately 19 hours a week until Thursday, February 29,1996.

Mark was responsible for preparing the reconciliations for bank accounts that The Summit holds at Chase Manhattan. The Summit holds approximately 16 separate accounts of varying complexity. Mark also worked on various reconciliations of balance sheet accounts.

Mark was always prompt, and worked diligently during his time with us.

Sincerely,
Susan W.
Accounting Manager

SUNY BROCKPORT

MEN"S & WOMEN"S SWIMMING & DIVING
Dr. Gregory A. K., Head Coach
B-323 Tuttle North
Brockport, New York 14420-2989
(585) 395-5344

To whom it may concern:

It is my pleasure to have been asked to write this letter of recommendation for Mark Russell. I have known about Mark's talent in diving for more than 25 years. Mark was one of the divers I coached in the first New York State Empire Games in 1978. He was a top diver in New York and later in college at Kentucky where he earned many awards such as most valuable diver, all conference, and the 110% award. Mark is a student of the sport of diving and he used his vast knowledge to successfully coach the SUNY Brockport divers during the 2002-03 season. He continually demonstrated his passion for the sport and his compassion for the divers throughout the season. He brought along two novice divers to a point where they were very competitive with seasoned divers in our conference. He was a tough task master who expected a 100% effort from the divers at all times, and succeeded in keeping them motivated to try more difficault dives over the course of the season.

Mark used all of our available diving aids including: the spotting rig, the weight room for strength and flexibility, and a variety of video tapes of established as well as taped sessions of our divers. He was one of the most enthusiastic diving coaches I have had working with our team. Mark brought a freshness to our practices that had been missing for some time. In our end-of- season evaluations the divers ranked him very highly on his knowledge, ability to break down dives, and determination to see them improve and be successful. I stated in my evaluation that Mark was a very dedicated, serious, hard-working coach who had as his primary goals the growth and success of the student/athletes in competition and the classroom.

Wherever Mark chooses to continue his coaching, I know he will be a strong asset to the program and the students. It is without reservation that I recommerd him to you.

Sincerely,
Dr. Gregory A. K.
Head Swimming and Diving Coach